D

How to be an Illustrator
Darrel Rees

Second Edition

Contents

Central Park by Romy Blümel

Foreword
Nicholas Blechman

Illustration is a stealthy sport. To win you need more than just talent. You need a hunter's instinct. You need to know the lay of the land. You need to know what publications exist, who publishes them, and how to get the publishers' attention. You have to lure your prey with exquisite work. All this may sound daunting, but this book will help.

Being an illustrator is not just about creating good art. There is also an art to being a successful illustrator. There exists an (until now) unwritten methodology on how to get clients and keep them. This handbook has invaluable information on how to survive in the publishing jungle. It contains all the dos and don'ts that never get covered in art school. Here is everything I would like to have known before I showed my portfolio – an envelope with loose photocopies and messy silkscreen prints – to legendary art director and design critic Steven Heller 26 years ago. I still got a job, but only one. Years of humiliation, rejection and frustration could have been avoided.

Art directors are the most important people for you. They are at the top of the food chain. You only have one or two chances to impress them. Being one myself, I am always shocked when I meet illustrators to review their portfolio by how easy it is to tell the student from the seasoned professional (hint: the student has an oversize portfolio with original art and no website; the pro has a small custom-made book with clean printouts and a functional site).

The future of illustration may seem uncertain, with newspaper readership declining and magazines tightening their belts. The number of new illustrators entering the field each year easily outnumbers the number of new magazines launched. Nevertheless, there will always be opportunities for new illustrators. Editorial art directors like myself are always looking for fresh talent. We are always trying to find new ways to communicate because we are often working with recurring topics (healthcare, the Iraq war, Chinese growth). To find new solutions, we need new illustrators. Nor is the field limited to editorial illustration: today's illustrators can apply their skills to graphic novels, online animation or the art scene. Illustrators no longer work in one area but a multiplicity of fields, and this is what makes being an illustrator today so exciting.

If there is anybody who knows about becoming an illustrator, it's Darrel Rees. Over the years he has brought together some of the finest illustrators under one umbrella. Heart not only represents a diverse range of some of the best new talent in the field, but also knows how to package illustration for art directors. Darrel is passionate about illustration, and this passion has been translated into this smart, useful and, not coincidentally, beautifully illustrated book.

Keep it by your drawing table.

Introduction
The broad and social church of illustration

Welcome to this second edition of *How to be an Illustrator*. This updated version is now in full colour and addresses some of the new developments in the six years since the first edition, notably the growth of social media and its role in promoting yourself and your work.

I still maintain that for most illustrators, a foundation of editorial work, followed by publishing, design and advertising work, remains a norm. Beyond that central field there are specialist areas that can be explored if your interest and your work is so inclined. I have interviewed practitioners active in those fields that are not my areas of expertise, such as gaming and interactive animation, children's books, 3D 'illustration', animation and natural history. There should be plenty of useful guidance with regard to work in these areas. Contracts, where they exist, will also vary greatly, as they will concern themselves with rights that are unique to those specialisms.

What will change in more traditional areas is of course the impact of the range of digital platforms now available and in development, such as the interactive possibilities for narrative and online versions of magazines, viewed via such devices as the iPad and Kindle.

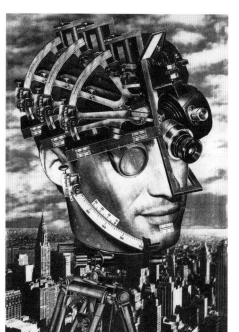

Self-initiated collage

I suspect that not all the visual content of an 'interactive' version of a magazine will necessarily be interactive or animated. The role an illustration plays for a feature article is primarily a supporting one. A moving image may prove distracting if one were trying to read a page of text. However, in the realms of advertorial or straightforward advertising content, the possibilities may well be explored and exploited more readily. Cost may be one factor where 'interactive' visuals are used, but it's also a matter of their function. A one-page 'ad' might be in effect a one-page movie screen, telling a product's story and brand through moving images.

Given these potential applications, the nature of illustration as we know it may well become less and less two-dimensional, or rather the three dimensions plus movement may be what changes the nature of the visuals and the language they speak.

The six years that have passed since this book was first published have seen much change in the modes of communication and, arguably, of self-promotion that one can apply. Possibly the greatest change is that the social media networks now play a greater role in the hunt for work for everyone, not just illustrators. However, what are the implications for the illustrator seeking to further a reputation and career?

Numerous artists successfully employ social media networks as part of their promotional strategy. I'll be looking at some of these individuals, to see how they make such networks work for them. They will share what they learned in the process to help you navigate a clearer path through social media networking.

As social media have gained ground, alongside what might be considered the 'traditional' website, the need for a physical portfolio of work has arguably diminished. I'll be looking at its place in the promotional arsenal as well as revisiting the manner in which work is commissioned and handled, and shifts in the working landscape within which illustrators operate.

The selection of artists featured in the book has changed, to reflect a broader spectrum of activity, and their work is reproduced in beautiful full colour. I'll be looking at how these individuals established themselves in their differing arenas as well as hearing what they might have done differently, having learned a few lessons along the way.

This book's aim remains the same: to be an invaluable resource to the reader in terms of understanding how the industry works from the bottom up. While each person's experience will vary, there are key pointers that will help you build solid foundations for your one-person business, which will help you establish yourself as an illustrator and maintain your activity in the longer term. Good foundations remain the basis of a viable career in illustration.

Chapter 1
Getting started

So, how do you become an illustrator?

> Thinking about everything you need to know as an illustrator can be overwhelming. The reality, of course, is that you pick things up as you go along. In this book I aim to give some guidance to those starting out, where I had none myself, but also to show how you learn what you need as and when you need it. Perhaps surprisingly, you can leave a BA or even an MA course without necessarily knowing how to bridge the gap between what you've been doing at college and the professional practice of an illustrator.

Where does simply drawing end and becoming an illustrator begin? Great drawing is always a pleasure to see, but good drawing does not necessarily make an illustrator. If you were to express professional illustration as a Venn diagram of requisite skills, good draughtsmanship could certainly be represented within that diagram but not necessarily as a dominating factor. Indeed, some illustrators 'can't draw' or choose not to for their commercial practice.

The presumption that drawing and illustration are one and the same thing is a common misconception, and one that an awful lot of art school graduates fall prey to. Most graduates, on leaving art college and being faced with the financial realities of supporting themselves, would like to earn some money in a related area of activity. Many have come to me as an agent and said that they would like to 'do a bit of illustration' to help make ends meet. Without touching on the arrogance implicit in this, the main problem is a failure to understand that different skills are required to create good commercial illustration.

To draw or not to draw

> My own experience in this area is pertinent. On leaving school and starting a foundation course, I began my art education as someone who did meticulously observed pencil drawings, painstakingly, over several days. In addition to submitting a portfolio of work, the entrance examination to what was then the Bath Academy of Art involved a 'drawing test'. You were required to take an apple, peel it, cut it into four parts, place these on a mirror, rest the knife in the apple, garnish all this

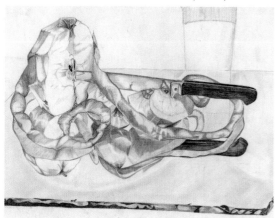

with the peel and then draw it as a still life. You were also asked to choose an everyday object and to draw it in four different ways to express different aspects. You needed to communicate its form, function and material of construction, and then to draw or write the name of the object in a way that expressed its function. The third and final part was drawing an A3 self-portrait (420 x 297mm/16.5 x 11.7in) and then a quarter of the face, also A3. At that time, this kind of drawing was precisely what I enjoyed and could tackle without any real problem. A year later, I wasn't drawing very much at all; I would even say I shied away from it. By the time I came to create illustrations, there was no drawing in them at all.

The 'drawing test' for art school

I think this move away from drawing was due to a very common experience people have on arriving at art school. The education you receive sets out to destroy all your assumptions, in an attempt to make you look afresh at how you observe, draw, paint and generally create images. It possibly allowed me to break away from the kind of still-life, observational pieces that I had been doing, but it was a full three years before I came back to drawing with anything approaching understanding, let alone any enjoyment, passion or commitment.

In the intervening years, I didn't 'get' drawing at all. It was a bit of a no-go area for me. Instead, I made collages – juxtaposing words and phrases with incongruous images in an attempt to represent a narrative of thoughts. Even before art school, I had found collage very engrossing, so returning to it, as an alternative to drawing, kick-started the evolution of my own visual vocabulary, which relied wholly on found images.

On returning to drawing, it felt very refreshing, and while I never felt inclined to work it into my illustrations – or 'artworks', such as they were – the very acts of observing and noting down involved in drawing (as well as deciding which bits of information to include and which to leave out) influenced how I put together images in my collages. When you are used to considering the weight or thickness of a line, or its dynamic in terms of speed or hesitancy, this kind of consideration helps in fine-tuning compositions.

The decision not to include drawing directly in my artworks was instinctive and purely personal. Most 'drawing' illustrators I know find that it is second nature and inherent in their drive to communicate. For me, a substitution had taken place, and drawing had probably always been about observing, rather than about narrating or communicating.

The illustrator's skill set

> A common question is, 'What do I need to become an illustrator?' Defining an illustrator's skill set isn't really about itemizing a practical set of abilities, such as manual dexterity, or being able to render figures or clouds beautifully. Rather, it is defined largely through the lens of the individual illustrator's personality. The personality brings the decision-making process, the ideas, notions and opinions, to a commission; the practical skills provide the means to express them. If you have the means to express such things, but nothing worth expressing, then those skills are fairly meaningless, aren't they?

There are plenty of arguments and counter-arguments about how much value should be placed on good draughtsmanship when looking at illustration. I know plenty of illustrators whose drawings are sublime. The drawing underpins what they do, but is not always as evident as you might expect. What is certain is that good drawing alone is not enough to make an illustrator. Without resorting to specific examples, which in any case could probably be countered by other examples, the best way I can articulate the quality of good drawing is to say that a beautifully produced and lifelike or credible representation could be said to be a 'good drawing'. However, a not particularly 'good drawing' judged by those defining principles might still be an effective 'signifier' as an illustration and, in that particular context, be a very good and interesting illustration. Furthermore, the choice of information provided by the drawing also impacts on its success or failure as an illustration.

An illustrator's 'skill', beyond his or her approach to drawing or style, could be said to lie in the decision-making process: what information should be included and what should be left out? Such decisions in turn are predicated on circumstances or parameters defined by the requirements of a design problem. An illustration can often transcend its original context, yet it has still been created to work within a predetermined design specification and in response to a specific brief.

Many other components of the illustrator's skill set could be said to be innate. While you can learn to be an illustrator, there are elements of the applied-art process that you really have to enjoy – things that you can't just do for the money. This is a little more difficult to articulate, but here goes.

Curiosity, expressed as an interest in almost any subject, is an important asset to an illustrator. Most illustrators (again, not all) handle a range of work across a wide spectrum of subject matter. Being able to read about an arcane piece of new financial legislation and understand how it will affect the average citizen sufficiently to have an opinion about it, or to be able to precis the core information as a visual explanation or metaphor, is a real skill. The alternative is to be the illustrator who dispassionately executes 'the editor's idea' rather than coming up with something more interesting yourself. Executing somebody else's occasionally mediocre idea is a soul-destroying experience – joyless and ultimately rather embarrassing. Occasionally you have no choice if you want to do the job, but in most cases art directors and editors will look at alternative ideas. In handling commissions, you will sometimes find that commissioners think they are being helpful by having a preconceived idea of what they want. You then have to explain that it may be best to let you, the illustrator, read the copy and come up with your own ideas.

A sense of humour goes a long way in the illustrator's skill set, both in coping with the trials and tribulations experienced along the way, and of course in putting a witty spin on an illustration job. I'm continually entertained by Matt Groening's metaphorical transpositions, links and references to films and notable events in *The Simpsons*. Having a broad frame of reference that encompasses books, films, mythology and current affairs helps in creating links that lead to witty solutions to visual problems.

I guess this is also the foundation for creative lateral thinking – the metaphorical leaps and cross-fertilized reference points that keep the illustrator's mind an agile, playful and creative tool.

Adjusting to freelance life

> Self-motivation is essential, although this is obviously not exclusive to the illustrator's skill set. Being self-employed or freelance isn't for everyone. There is ever-present uncertainty, even once you are established, as work can dry up at any point. I doubt anyone is immune to this. What comes with experience, though, is the ability to ride the ebb and flow and not panic when there's no work.

Even in the first few years of working as an illustrator, I was lucky enough to be continually busy, but I found that for three consecutive years work seemed to dry up at the same point in the year, for four to six weeks.

When it happens, the first week of being quiet is a blessing. It allows you to take a breather, clear up the studio and tackle that long-neglected admin. In the second week you may start to feel a little twitchy, and by week three you can convince yourself that your career is over and the phone will never ring again. It took me about three years to relax into the periods of no work. You can't afford to be complacent but, equally, panicking doesn't help. I think of it as walking along a path you can't see; you need to have confidence that the path is there and keep walking. As I had never been employed, I was not used to a monthly salary, so working freelance became the norm. I've known designers who, having worked for major consultancies, tried to go freelance but were unable to cope with both the uncertainty and having expenses, such as couriers and materials, coming out of their own pocket. As you develop your own career, it's probably harder to give up financial security for uncertainty than to start with no certainty other than faith in your own ability.

Choosing illustration   **>** While I was defining the skill set of an illustrator, I realized that I had no conscious understanding of it when I started out. In fact, I had no real plan to be an illustrator.

In my final year of a visual communications degree, I wanted a new challenge, and the idea of applying to the Royal College of Art, London, seemed audacious. Having spoken to a tutor who advised me to perhaps leave it for a year, I thought, no, let's just do this and see what happens. I applied for the graphics course at the RCA, which at the time roughly mirrored the diversity of the course I was following at Bath Academy. I had no thought then of becoming an illustrator. I wanted to be a graphic designer, creating visual solutions while using elements of typography in my work. I loved type forms, but was frankly awful at typography. At that point, at the risk of sounding truly archaic, type classes consisted of tracing letter forms using a rapidograph. It was a slow, tedious process, fatal to any kind of spontaneity. Always an impatient type, I preferred getting into the letterpress room, inking up woodblock type and printing the letters on to images using a proofing press.

At the RCA, I struggled with graphics, which I found to be 20 per cent idea and 80 per cent laborious fiddling and fine-tuning. This wasn't helped by my lack of core typographic skills. I opted for fun, flip solutions to projects, expressed in the form of roughly assembled visuals. My heart sank when I was asked to go away and clean it all up and 'finish' it. I simply was not cut out for the rigours of graphic design. You need patience and a fastidious nature and, frankly, that wasn't me.

My 'eureka' moment came via two meetings I had at the RCA. I had encountered Alan Fletcher of Pentagram very briefly at a private view at the college; he had agreed to see me and my portfolio if I gave him a call. I duly went along and showed him my work, but made the mistake of telling him how unsure I was

Guy Marshall

Creative Director, StudioSmall

Can you briefly outline your career path?

> Degree from Preston Polytechnic, Designer, The Chase, Williams and Phoa, Imagination. I set up StudioSmall in 2004.

What was your first experience of working with an illustrator?

> Being taught by Martin Chatterton at Preston Poly. It was a really good experience. I did have a phase of trying to draw like Martin, but I think that was a bit of an ask for me.

Why and when do you choose to call on the services of illustration?

> It's completely driven by the client and their brief.

Do you keep a stable of illustrators that you turn to frequently?

> We have a set we really like; we also have ones we really want to work with.

Where do you look for new talent?

> Agents, magazines, my kids' bookshelves.

What do you feel are illustration's strengths?

> It has the ability to communicate complex subjects with real imagination; often a photograph would be impossible to shoot.

How do you find working with an illustrator?

> They always bring a viewpoint that is different to ours, which is why we like working with them.

Do you ever have to reject artwork? On what grounds?

> We have asked for radical changes but never all-out rejection. You have to work together to get the right result.

What kind of promotional items work best for you?

> PDFs work, but meeting agents/artists is best for me. I'd much rather meet than get anything in the post. Lots of e-mails are a bit of a pain. Postcards tend to head to the bin.

Do you see many illustrators with their portfolios?

> We see lots, and have four or five agents we will see every year. Everyone finds the same people online. Meeting the person gives you a view on their potential as a partner on a project.

What is your experience of illustrators' websites?

> It's like shopping online. I'd prefer to see the work in person, but often time does not permit. Ease of access is key for me, and an image size we can print out to show a client is always helpful. Negatives include too much web design, small pictures, complex navigation.

What do you feel about working via an agent?

> First point of call when we are thinking about a commission, they know their stuff and have a good eye. They are often good sounding boards. I like agents when the client has a decent budget; it keeps everything clear.

What do you feel about fees?

> Very good value given the time, attention to detail and love required. We try to be transparent – the client requires value for money but the artist needs to eat.

How do you feel about contracts taking copyright?

> Tricky. I guess it depends how much money was paid.

What would prevent you recommissioning?

> Late work, busted budgets, unhappy clients (none of which we have had).

What do you think is the future of illustration?

> The world still has a massive appetite for imagination and craft. If you can make that move in some way, you are on to a winner.

Offer advice to a new illustrator.

> Martin Chatterton told me never miss a deadline. Don't do the same image over and over again: it gets boring.

about my suitability for a career in graphic design, and that I wasn't sure where I was going. (I still find this a perfectly reasonable admission.) He looked at me in a very irritated way and said, 'How old are you? And you still don't know what you want to be doing?' The conversation ended there and I left feeling pretty stupid.

The second meeting was with a commissioning art director from Penguin Books, Cherriwyn Magill, whom I knew because she occasionally taught at Bath. Her take on the portfolio was a good deal more helpful. She understood the area of graphic design that interested me, but summed up by saying that such work was 'thin on the ground', and that it would be hard to make a living from it. What I had, she told me, was really an illustration portfolio.

Quite simply, that was when I chose to become an illustrator, something that had not really occurred to me before. Once I knew what I was supposed to be doing, things quickly came into focus. Without the clear opinions of this tutor and working professional, I might have floundered around between the design and illustration camps, being neither fish nor fowl and wasting a lot of time and energy.

Gathering advice   **>** While at college, you may well find that you get conflicting, often completely contradictory, opinions from tutors – clear-sighted advice can be hard to come by. I would say that one of the key things you need to be able to do by the time you graduate is think for yourself. Don't try to please every tutor, and do learn to shrug off opinions about your work that you don't necessarily agree with. The problem is that this is, in itself, a delicate balancing act; if you don't listen, process, consider and weigh up advice from other people, you will be in danger of learning nothing. You have to be open to constructive criticism and guidance, but ultimately confident enough to make your own mind up. When asking a tutor's advice about how suitable your portfolio is for a career in illustration – or any other associated area of art and design – you need to talk to the tutor whose opinion and advice you respect and trust the most. This won't necessarily be the one who is most friendly to you, who is unlikely to tell you uncomfortable truths. Ultimately, the advice you're given will either chime with something you instinctively feel or it won't. There are no clear pathways here unfortunately. The bottom line is, if you have a tutor you trust, ask for an opinion, but try not to go to everyone asking the same question, trying to make a decision by committee.

I began showing my portfolio to art directors at the end of my second year at the RCA – it was still a three-year MA at that point. My first job came with my second meeting. Debi Angel, who was then art director at *Elle* magazine, was well known for trying out new illustrators and giving people their first breaks. I came away with my first commission, due in a week's time. After the initial euphoria passed I was terrified; I had never been under as serious a deadline as a magazine going to press. Would I get it done in time? Would it be good enough?

A week later, I delivered a collage that was a metre (three feet) high and half a metre (20 inches) wide. Debi was delighted with the piece, but wondered how it would fit on a drum scanner. (This was something of an ironic problem, given that the piece was to be reproduced at a height of 5cm (2 in) in the gutter margin.) When the magazine came out a month later, I was as proud as can be.

Preparing at college   **>** I consider myself very lucky in that by the time I left college I had already received seven commissions, with each one generating more work. Things snowballed from there, really. While this was from a master's course, I think that regardless of whether you're an undergraduate or a graduate, there are things you can do to prepare the ground for your career post-college.

Portfolio preparation and research are the two most obvious steps, along with building a website. Putting together a portfolio will probably be part of your graduation preparations; using facilities while they are free, or less expensive, is a bit of forward thinking you'll be grateful for later. Similarly, start working out your promotional system so you're ready to get everything rolling when you leave.

Looking at potential editorial and publishing clients via publications and books available in bookstores is an obvious way to acquaint yourself with what is going on in the world of design and illustration. You can also glean a lot of names from this activity.

Even before leaving college, you should pay attention to the kinds of illustration used by magazines and publishers, and see which publications are likely to be interested in your kind of work. Being curious and researching actively and professionally are two sides of the same coin. The former is a low-intensity process of absorbing what is going on, almost by osmosis; the latter is more proactive and requires organization. It's the difference between a hobby and a business.

Since you are getting everything ready for graduation, your portfolio has to be sorted out anyway, so why not give a few people a call while you are still at college to see if you can get in to see them? It's what you'll have to do soon enough anyway, so why not get stuck in?

Contacts   **>** Without asking your tutor for his or her entire database of clients, you can ask them if they could recommend people to whom you could show your portfolio. Make sure you ask a tutor who is also a 'practitioner', as opposed to one who may no longer have much meaningful contact with the industry. If they give you the name and phone number of one person who will see you on their recommendation, then you've made a good start. If you ask each person you meet in this way to recommend someone who might be interested in seeing your work, you slowly build a network. And if each person you see gives you, say, two names, then very quickly your list of contacts builds in pyramid form.

Bear in mind that asking for contacts can be a delicate matter. Some people may sidestep such a request if they are not too confident of the reception you or your portfolio will get. How you will be received reflects back on the person who made the recommendation. If someone I trust asks me to see an illustrator with his or her portfolio, out of respect for that person I probably will, but in the expectation that it will be interesting and not a waste of time. If someone consistently sends me people whose work is good and/or interesting, I am likely to carry on seeing the illustrators they recommend. If, however, the recommendations are patchy and I end up seeing a lot of mediocre work, I'm likely to be reluctant to carry on seeing the people they recommend, and will begin to question their judgement.

'The most daunting aspect was to find myself doing work with no one around who could give me an opinion – no tutors, no students ... I hadn't realized that being an illustrator could be such a lonely job.'

Aude Van Ryn, Illustrator

Going to social events where you can meet clients or practising illustrators, or both, in a relaxed atmosphere is also helpful in building up contacts. Apart from smaller group or individual private views, events run by illustration societies and others are a magnet for clients and illustrators, so try to get along to them. In many cases you need to join these societies in order to get access to their events, but it's probably worthwhile as they will generally also provide guidance and information, including legal advice, lists of agents, and so on.

In attending such events as private views, try to avoid walking up to people with your information-seeking agenda on your sleeve; just try to be sociable. If you meet someone at a private view, get along with them and, by the end of the evening, you should know who they are and where they work, so that you can go away and find a phone number for them. Calling up and saying, 'Hi, we met the other night at so-and-so PV. Would you be able to make time to see me with my portfolio as I'd appreciate some advice?' is likely to be better received than badgering them at a relaxed private view until you get their number and a vague promise to see you and your book – in which case you're more likely to be remembered as a nuisance and best avoided. If you can just meet people and chat in a relaxed atmosphere, you're more likely to be *given* offers of help. Most illustrators I know are friendly and helpful; if they see a sincere and smart newcomer who needs a bit of advice, they are generous with their time and information. If they feel hounded, they're more likely to clam up and avoid you.

The economic realities

> I hit the ground running and have been fortunate enough to have worked consistently and supported myself via illustration work solidly since college. However, for some illustrators who came out of the RCA only two years after me, the story was quite different. The difference was not that I was a 'better' illustrator than they were; rather, it was down to external circumstances beyond our control. I left college during an economic boom, but two years later a rather nasty recession hit. I was lucky enough to get the wind beneath my wings, which gave me a flying start, while these illustrators graduated into a much tougher economic climate and consequently never quite got that start. They had an uphill struggle to establish themselves, and it took longer for them to achieve any kind of financial stability.

Another external factor that affects a young would-be illustrator is the amount of debt most students are now saddled with on leaving college. The pressure to get a job in order to support yourself in the short term is very real, but can ultimately be a distraction. You are, after all, a new graduate for one year only. Then a new round of graduates emerges and you are 'downgraded' to 'recent graduate'.

Another year later, you're just one of a swelling throng of budding illustrators trying to make a living. Nobody hands out badges with these labels, but you need to make the most of your 'debut' appearance. There may be 50 graduates from your college. Two years later, that's 150 job-hungry graduates from your college alone, so you need to be determined and committed, as soon as you leave college, to make an impact as soon as possible.

You've spent four intense years of study – thinking about, eating, sleeping and breathing illustration. To keep up that momentum, you need to keep doing so. If you spend a year working on something completely different, your portfolio won't move forward and you probably won't do much drawing or picture-making, so it can be hard to get back into the swing of it. You will have to try to rejoin a fast-flowing river of new graduates in the search for work. There are probably examples of great illustrators who did something else in between leaving college and 'becoming an illustrator', but they are likely to be in the minority. You have to make your own decisions about how you want to spend your time, but bear in mind the risks involved in not getting on with your illustration career straight away.

Location, location > In the UK, illustration remains a very London-centric business. In the US, New York is the main centre, with its large number of publishing houses and design and advertising agencies. However, given the size of the country, there are other hubs. Los Angeles, San Francisco and Chicago all have a lot of opportunities for illustrators – they are major metropolises, and most of the leading advertising agencies will have offices in these cities. In France, it is certainly a Paris-centric business; in other European countries, most illustration activity is centred around the capital or the main city for publishing (Frankfurt in Germany, for example).

These days you should, in theory, be able to work from anywhere via e-mail and the internet. Once you're established, this is a possibility, and many of the artists I deal with are based outside London and New York. The problem for those beginning an illustration career is the need to get themselves noticed, their work seen and clients calling, and this is done most effectively from within their country's illustration centre. I'm a great believer in personal contact; illustrators starting their careers need to get out there and meet people. However, if your work has enough focus and is at a stage where it can attract the attention of an agent, a base away from a major centre can be viable, provided the agent is proactive with you and your work. If you're simply added to an already bulging roster of artists at the agency, and left to wait for interest to come to you, it's not a real alternative. I'll be looking at how you go about choosing the right kind of agent and the general pros and cons of having one in Chapter 8.

A juggling act > Usually, living in an 'illustration hub' means you are living in an economically very active and vibrant city. Consequently, it probably isn't cheap, which adds to your financial pressures while you are trying to get some commissioned work and be creative. If your only option is to have a day job, you need to be organized.

If an illustration commission comes up while you are committed to a day job, then, even if there is a degree of flexibility, you will still have to work to a deadline, which may not fit comfortably with your job. Physically doing the illustration is not necessarily the hard part; allowing for late-night working, you can probably manage that. But getting 'roughs' or sketches to someone and being available to hear feedback from the client can be more difficult. If you're lucky, you may get feedback on the spot, but if not, it might be a day or two later, depending on the chain of decision-making involved in the commission.

Your mobile will be an obvious aid. With a smartphone you can access your e-mail on the go. Getting a rough or sketch to a client is easier than ever nowadays, via e-mail and services such as YouSendIt and Dropbox. You can also scan a rough of your work using your phone instead of a scanner, for uploading or e-mailing. If you can't scan your rough, you can always rely on the good old fax machine. A fax may seem archaic, but people still draw with pen and pencil on paper. Checking these things out in advance, and knowing you have the facilities you need at hand, can go a long way to reducing your stress levels if you take on a commission that you have to juggle with a day job.

Reference and sourcing

> Access to reference material is a good deal easier than it used to be, thanks to Google. That said, if you're a collagist like me, there are issues concerning both quality of resolution and copyright. If you're simply trying to find out what something looks like, then Google is fine. As a point of principle, I think illustrators should be sourcing reference material continually, building up their own library. Not only is this a matter of not relying on Google, but it's about having more personal and eclectic source material, which should contribute to the uniqueness of your work.

A helpful tip from someone who didn't impose order on his own collection: organize your reference material! Being a collagist whose work is largely based on found items and bits of torn packaging, I spent most of my time walking around, with my head down, looking out for bits of colourful rubbish. When I got home, I emptied my pockets or bag into a big black rubbish sack in the corner of my room – this was my repository of collage material. It was obviously a bad habit to get into; as my work changed to incorporate certain elements relevant to the subject of an illustration, images I sourced specifically still ended up being 'filed' in that bin bag in the corner. I had a good memory for the images I had, so the system – such as it wasn't – worked reasonably well.

Then one day I came back from a two-week break with a half-finished job to complete on that same day. Two weeks was long enough for my mind to have misplaced all the elements I needed, and that day was one of the most stressful I can remember. I went out the next morning and bought a dozen foolscap files and plastic sleeves, and set about roughly categorizing and filing the reference material I had amassed over three years or so. It made life immeasurably easier and allowed me to tackle short-deadline jobs with the minimum of stress.

Compiling your database

> Apart from the practicalities of executing an illustration commission while doing a day job, there are other aspects you need to consider organizing, which will help you to establish your illustration career while holding down a day job to pay the bills. There's the question of compiling a database of clients (be it in an address book or notebook, or using a database program on your computer) as well as keeping potential clients aware of your existence and availability for work.

Compiling a database is a matter of keeping useful information in an accessible form. How detailed it is depends on you and your needs at a given point in your career. Basic information includes company or publication name; name of your contact and their position at that company or publication; the address and telephone and fax numbers; and e-mail address. That's the minimum of information, and it should be searchable via contact or company name. It's also useful to include a field where you can note what piece of promo the contact has been sent and on what date. Consider a field to record the last time you met them, the last time they commissioned you, or even the last time they called in a portfolio of yours. A further field is useful to record such things as fees/rates paid for work that you do for that person, plus anything else that's noteworthy. If they've moved recently and you worked with them previously, you can track the history of your working relationship with them. I also find it useful to note the last time the information on each person was checked or updated. A small database may initially be quite intimate, in that it's largely concerned with people you've had some contact with; in that case, noting when it was last updated is probably less relevant. If you have a bigger database with lots of people you don't have regular contact with, it is worth updating and checking the information every three to six months, to avoid wasting promotional items on someone who is no longer at a particular company.

Your calling card

> The traditional method of letting clients know about your work is a postcard featuring one of your images. Many people have these printed as part of their graduation show. It's a great opportunity to get your first promotional item printed in readiness for potential clients. The choice of image is very important, and you can easily waste the opportunity by choosing a personal favourite without considering that choice objectively. Few people, particularly when they are relatively inexperienced, are the best judges of their own work. It's easy to get too close to that favourite piece, print it as your postcard and then regret it. Everyone has to get used to making their own judgement calls eventually, particularly by the end of a degree course in which you may have been bombarded with contradictory opinions from different tutors. However, it's advisable to ask some of your peers and a tutor you trust for their opinions on which image would best represent what you are about and what the rest of your portfolio looks like. Normally, I'd be averse to the notion of a committee decision, but in this instance it might prove helpful. (When an art director shows an illustration around the office for opinion before getting back to you, I think it's indicative of weak decision-making. Ask a bunch of people about an image and they'll probably try to outdo each other in a competition for supercilious or facile comments. It's rarely a true measure of whether an illustration is working or not.)

With a bit of forward planning, your postcard can be used in conjunction with a website, which you can hopefully put together while still at college. Your approach to creating a website needs careful consideration too, but I'll deal with that in Chapter 6. In the meantime, that postcard can carry the web address and all your other contact details. If the image is a strong hook, it will lead those potential commissioners to your website where, hopefully, their interest will be rewarded with many more of your engaging images.

Once you've graduated and are juggling a day job with your nascent illustration career, you may find the cost of getting an updated postcard printed prohibitive in the face of making enough money to pay your rent and other bills. Running out images digitally on your printer at postcard size on heavier weight papers will work if you pay attention to detail, and either lay out several images on a page or carefully trim them down to postcard size and take care over how you provide your contact details. These can be typeset and printed digitally on the reverse or on labels, or you can use a rubber stamp. Every detail creates an impression, so make sure it's the impression you want to make.

Provided the quality of your work is consistently high, you can send out new images every month. If money is tight, send them to just a small handful of clients, but keep plugging away. It's a matter of getting your illustration career off the ground – at cottage-industry level to begin with if

Some examples of promotional postcards I've produced

necessary, but 'cottage industry' doesn't mean it can't reflect your originality and professionalism. If you have more money, or you have an inclination to invest some borrowed money in your nascent career, then you can obviously scale up your approach.

Together, your beginner's database and your simple promotional approach represent your career 'grow bag'. The whole process of shifting from being a passionate enthusiast to a passionate and enthusiastic professional is a gradual one. I found that I learned more in a month of working than I did in a year at college. This could be a personal failing on my part, but I think dealing with immovable, unavoidable commercial print deadlines focuses decision-making in the creative process, while the necessity to work concurrently on a number of commissions, with wildly different subject matters, means you automatically start to time-manage yourself. If it didn't come naturally at college, this will have to be learned swiftly if you are to survive.

Having looked at the nature of 'the right stuff' you need to be an illustrator, we need to address what to think about in preparing a portfolio – the 'rabbit in the hat' for face-to-face meetings with those people in a position to commission you.

Aude Van Ryn

How well do you think college prepared you for the realities of working as an illustrator?

> I came to England from Belgium for a foundation course at Brighton, moved to London to do a BA in Graphic Design and Illustration at Central Saint Martins, then did an MA in Illustration at the Royal College of Art. The MA gave me confidence and better access to professionals in illustration and design through visiting artists, tutors, lecturers. It was a challenging time as the level of students' work, as well as tutors' expectations, was very high. It certainly pushed me to experiment and produce more work.

Can you tell me anything about your first experiences on leaving college?

> Luckily, I was able to take a trip to Central and South America. This delayed the stress of being self-employed. I came back full of energy and ideas, having filled many sketchbooks with drawings, and was ready to carry on the pace even though work was not yet coming in. For the first, very quiet two years I set my own projects to stay busy and focused.

Were there things you found surprising or difficult in beginning work?

> The most daunting aspect was to find myself doing work with no one around who could give me an opinion – no tutors, no students … A lot of friends from college had moved away so I had no feedback on work I was producing, which took a while to get used to.

I also hadn't realized that being an illustrator can be such a lonely job.

How did you cope financially?

> I was fortunate, as my parents supported me through college. Afterwards, with their help, I bought a run-down house that was separated into two flats. I rented out one and lived on that income for the first three years.

Are you methodical in your working life?

> It's important to be. It allows you to work on several jobs at once without too much confusion, and deliver work on time. Admin is usually easy but needs to be done regularly. The hardest thing by far is to be self-employed and a mother at the same time. Constantly juggling work and family leaves very little time for anything else.

Do you work from home or a studio?

> I work from a studio shared with illustrators, graphic designers, architects and photographers. It is an inspiring environment. Getting out of the house and into the studio helps to put me in the 'work' mood. It's a community of people. Some of us have been sharing the space for a long time so we know each other pretty well. We share ideas, facilities, food and sometimes even jobs.

Do you have an agent?

> Yes. It alleviates the painstaking task of finding potential clients. I am supported on a regular basis and it's good to be part of a group of artists. The agent also has a different perspective on work and can help me focus on what

can be achieved. Not having to deal directly with clients about the financial side is also a relief! Also, I don't produce promotional material apart from a Christmas card – my agent produces material on a regular basis. The number of commissions coming in has increased in the last few years so it seems to work fine.

Can you imagine working without an agent?

> No! I would need to regularly update a website, send out promotional material, meet potential clients, deal with contracts, chase money. It would mean a far bigger workload.

Have you had any bad experiences with clients?

> I am generally very patient and flexible with clients, but it does happen on rare occasions. The last was a client from a cosmetic company who had used one of my illustrations as a test piece. He had reworked the image himself and wanted me to copy what he'd done. I refused and lost the job.

Have you ever turned work down for reasons other than not being available?

> Yes, recurring themes that I don't feel like illustrating any more, badly paid jobs or jobs that don't seem realistic given the work involved and time allowed.

What would be your one tip to a new illustrator?

> Be ambitious but realistic about what you want to achieve and have conviction in what you do. Sorry – this makes it three – but, last but not least, be prolific.

Illustrators: Aude Van Ryn

Left: *Therapist* for *Therapy Today*
Below: *Teenage Violence* for *Therapy Today*

Top left: For *Therapy Today*
Above left: *New Scientist* cover on the
theme of pollution
Above right: Brochure for City Circ

Chapter 2
Preparing your portfolio

> A portfolio is a portable sample case containing a representative selection of your best work. This is what you take to meetings with prospective clients to show them what you do and are hoping they will buy. It should show your USP, or 'unique selling point', whatever it may be, to its best advantage.

You will have a certain amount of work ready to show when you leave college. It's a matter of selecting which pieces are suitable for inclusion in your portfolio, to be shown to prospective art buyers, and which pieces can and should be left out. Thereafter, it's a question of presenting the work in the best way to maximize the impact of, and interest in, what you have to show.

Getting in to see clients with a portfolio is often difficult, and I would say that it is becoming more so. One of the reasons for this is that people are extremely busy and many feel they can check things out online without having to find time for a meeting with a person they don't know. With the growing plethora of online viewing options – websites, blogs, Tumblr, Flickr etc. – it would be easy to presume that there's little point in meeting people face to face, certainly for the person commissioning the illustration. From their point of view there are a lot of negatives. Having someone come in with their portfolio is a gamble. Even when an art director has received samples that piqued their interest, it is always possible that the quality of the portfolio isn't going to live up to that initial impression. Add to that the potential discomfort of a meeting where the illustrator either says too much, or doesn't say anything at all. The situation is often compounded by the commissioner having to be as positive as possible while getting the artist out of the door with a sigh of relief.

However, I would say that most commissioners of illustration like meeting illustrators. If they don't do it, it's simply a case of not having enough time, and they can generally see what they need to online. Many still make time because meeting the person behind the work can often provide insights into the work, as well as perhaps offer reassurance and confidence that the illustrator is an individual who can be relied on and is easy to work with.

In the case of editorial work, there is a limited risk for the commissioner, and most illustrators will do the bulk of their editorial work without meeting their client face to face. A body of work, be it online or in a physical portfolio, will either display a certain confidence of execution that will overcome any doubts a would-be commissioner might have, or appear not quite fully formed and resolved, and that's where a meeting could make a difference. For new illustrators, it often takes time to establish a body of work with a solid foundation, and that's sometimes about having 'live' working opportunities with which to prove themselves.

If you've managed to get yourself a meeting, you need to make the most of it. With this in mind, you need to interest the client in the work you are presenting, hold their attention and, hopefully, leave them thinking that it was a memorable encounter (for the right reasons). The need to surprise and bring depth to your work via the portfolio is now greater than ever before. The act of showing a spread of work is now increasingly fulfilled by web pages. The folio might show some work for context, but it needs to show, perhaps, some original drawings, choice sketchbook elements, work in development and so on. This range of work needs to be structured within the portfolio, somewhat like an essay. You need to avoid the 'story' of the portfolio jumping around from one thing to another, so try to give it a narrative flow where any sketchbook work or work in development acts as a supporting background to more resolved, 'finished' pieces.

I appreciate that this kind of expectation ratchets up the pressure, but a bit of preparation should allow both you and the client to enjoy the meeting and come away from it feeling positive. You need to leave the potential client with the best possible impression of you and your work. Take them to a peak and leave them there; don't take them all the way to that peak and then allow the meeting to slither downhill.

A good first impression can wither on the vine for a number of reasons, be it too much material to look at, or talking too much and generally outstaying your welcome. Think about the person who has given up his or her time to meet you and look at your work. Empathy is a key factor in interpersonal relationships. If you concentrate too much on what you want, without sparing a thought for the client's perspective, you can do yourself a huge disservice.

Any meeting can get off to a bad start if the presentation of the portfolio is ill-considered. No one should notice the portfolio more than the work itself. This applies as much to fussy, idiosyncratic and so-called original approaches to portfolios as to cheap, poorly fitting and badly presented ones.

Problem portfolios > I recently had someone come in to show a portfolio with a view to us representing him. I had seen his website and it was quite impressive – I was looking forward to the meeting and to talking to the person responsible for the work. The reality was disastrous. The would-be illustrator showed up with an A2 portfolio (594 x 420mm/23.4 x 16.5in), which can either excite you at the possibility of seeing some interesting originals, or fill you with dread at what might come out of it. In this case, the portfolio was filled with loose bits of mountboard (most far smaller than A2), each with a colour printout stuck to it and trimmed to the edge of the image. I tried to concentrate on the work but my irritation at the mode of presentation, particularly when compared to the website, just kept rising.

At the end of the 'presentation', I asked the illustrator how many clients he had been to see with his portfolio. He replied that perhaps six people had viewed the portfolio, but that the work he had received to date had come via his website. I then calmly explained to him how irritated I had become while trying to look at the work. I also took the time to explain that I was telling him this so that he had the opportunity to address the very evident problems in his presentation before he sank his own boat. I suggested that it looked as though someone had taken down a card-mounted exhibition and dropped it all into a carrying case, and he confessed that this was exactly what he had done. He had graduated two summers ago and been given a handful of commissions, but had not bothered to sort out his portfolio. The poor guy looked embarrassed, but I suggested an alternative approach and offered to see him again, if only to check that he had sorted out his presentation before he saw anyone else. It remains to be seen whether he'll come back, but it was a stark example of the impression you can create with a shoddily assembled, ill-considered portfolio.

Another recent meeting started worryingly when the illustrator showed me a selection of drawings made when he was eight years old. Fortunately, we moved swiftly on to some stunning work. The meeting, while very successful because of the quality of the work, still left me with the feeling that it had peaked after about 15 minutes. Thereafter, it was a further 45 minutes of hard work for diminishing returns. Too much material to look at lessened the impression created by the first 15 minutes of portfolio page-turning. Unfortunately, I was glad when the meeting ended, which was a shame and wholly avoidable.

In anticipating how you would like a meeting to go, consider the impression you are trying to make. Aim to create that impression succinctly by preparing your portfolio with thought and care. It is tempting to show everything, blinding the prospective viewer with quantity rather than quality. There is no point in treating this like a meeting with your college tutor, who was being paid to look at your work and give guidance on as many aspects of it, including your approach to it, as possible, because a prospective client isn't. The two meetings I mentioned above were examples of bad presentation and poor editing, respectively. The first was disastrous; the second unnecessarily left me with a diminished impression of a good body of work. (Fortunately for that person the work really was stunning, and this tipped the balance in his favour. Few are that fortunate.)

Guidelines

Content
> Asking yourself a couple of simple questions will focus your preparation. What do you want the portfolio to say about you and your work? What, as a potential client, would you want from someone's portfolio? Thinking about it from the potential viewer's perspective helps you to define the parameters of your presentation.

As a basic wish list, you want your portfolio to show that you are professional and therefore reliable – someone who can be trusted to produce an image of quality and originality, that meets the brief you've been given, by the agreed deadline.

I appreciate that this can sound a little earnest and po-faced, but it is the subtext, the tacit understanding, that needs to come through when someone views your portfolio. This is the cornerstone of its message. Thereafter, it's about the creative spark, your originality and the portfolio's ability to inspire your audience, hitting them with the 'Wow!' factor that will leave them wanting to commission you on the spot.

Unless you don't have much work, and every piece you do have is inarguably brilliant, you'll need to show an edited selection. This should emphasize a reasonably clear direction in your illustration and show what you've been doing to its best advantage. You may have what appear to be several different approaches to your work and, if so, you'll need to handle how this is shown (if at all) very carefully. An illustrator's approach and style can take time to evolve and become personal, but in the meantime showing diverse approaches in order to 'fish', seeing which one people are most interested in, is probably not a good idea. There are thousands of illustrators out there, so having a bit of this and a bit of that to your name is not going to help you get a job. Why would anyone commission someone who does 'a bit' of a particular kind of illustration? If they know what they want, they can choose between a handful of people who specialize in just that. You don't want to create the impression of being a jack-of-all-trades; rather, ensure that you are the master of one.

There is probably an optimum number of pages in a portfolio, ranging, I would say, from 20 to 40 sides or pages. Twenty might be a little on the thin side but, if the quality is consistent, would be about right for someone just starting out. If you are particularly prolific and have enough good-quality work, go for the upper end of the range. Much beyond 40 pages and things can get repetitive or simply too long-winded, and you risk losing the viewer's attention.

Whether you're showing 20 or 40 pages, you need to pace the portfolio. This is really an instinctive judgement and one you learn to make with time and experience. No matter how much you edit a body of work to the core high-quality selection, within that you will still find a hierarchy of the most successful pieces. The aim of pacing the portfolio is to ensure that it flows, rather than jumps around, and that it generates impact and interest. These will inevitably rise or fall as someone works through the book, but it's up to you to orchestrate the points where they rise and fall, and to ensure the book finishes on a high note. You don't want a portfolio that starts well and goes downhill towards the end. So, spread out the high notes and pace the work between those anchors.

Context
> If you have work that is based on a text, be it a book, poem or magazine article, be prepared to explain this in a concise way. You don't necessarily need to show the mocked-up text; if the surrounding text layouts are badly designed, they can do more damage to your work than not having any at all. What the reference to a book or article will do, however, is show that your work can articulate ideas or opinions on a given text, which is part of the illustrator's job description.

In their early days of working, most people show some 'tear-sheets', i.e. printed pages featuring their work in the context of a magazine spread. Similarly, flat printed copies of book covers can be used, either trimmed to show only the front, or in their entirety if the work features on the back cover as well. The potential downside to this is that the page or cover may not be well laid out, or may feature visually messy ads. Printed pages can also yellow and age quickly and can make a portfolio look messy. If a tear-sheet is from a magazine or

A spread from Aude Van Ryn's portfolio showing various images and one tear-sheet

newspaper job, the date in the corner of the page can age the work prematurely, particularly if it's one of your stronger pieces.

You can get around some of these problems by asking the original client if they can give you a high-resolution PDF of the page with your image in context. You can then print it out at whatever size you want, cropping extraneous matter where desirable and possible. This gives you the option to show the page to your work's best advantage. Alternatively, print a small example of the image in context, to feature alongside a clean print of it on its own.

Another way of dealing with printed samples or tear-sheets is to keep examples of a few favourite printed pieces, still in their publications, in the back of the portfolio, and feature only the images themselves in its main body.

I would agree with the logic of showing that you've had work commissioned and printed by featuring it in context, in some form or other. However, once you've done a reasonable amount of work, you can concentrate on showing the images themselves, retaining only a few favourite, well-designed, well-printed examples of your work in context.

Sketchbooks
> Much as it's tempting to show sketchbooks, be very selective. I've seen sketchbooks that are chock-full of imaginative scribblings – nascent ideas that tie in with the main body of work. They can show a viewer how the illustrator thinks. I've seen many more sketchbooks that are filled with meaningless scribbles, 'notes to self' and poor drawings of friends sitting around a student house; frankly, those aren't going to impress anyone. If you have a sketchbook

that contains a mix of good and bad, think about extracting the wheat from the chaff and including the best bits in the folio to back up other pieces of work. Scan these images and print them out on decent quality paper; they are then a valuable addition. Even if you have several sketchbooks of great drawings and scribblings to back up your portfolio, it's advisable to have only one in the portfolio, and to offer it as an optional part of the viewing; if you have great stuff nestling in sketchbooks, consider scanning and printing them so that they play a larger role in the portfolio.

Originals or prints?

> Since work ultimately ends up printed or appearing digitally on screen, showing the originals as a default position is unnecessary. If originals exist, art directors or would-be commissioners are generally interested in seeing 'the real thing', as it gives them a clearer insight into how you work and what the quality of the mark-making is like. However, beyond providing a taster of what your originals look like, showing them should not be at the expense of a good, clearly presented portfolio.

Scans and printouts can work very well, because they enable you to design the portfolio. Being able to decide the size at which your images appear on the pages, and whether the pages are consistently designed — i.e. all on the same kind of paper, full bleed to the portfolio page, and so on — is a huge benefit. It assists you in pacing the flow of the portfolio, as full-page images can be followed by smaller ones grouped together on the next page. This helps to maintain the dynamism of your presentation.

A view of Tom Gauld's portfolio

The 'casing' – what kind of portfolio? > You have numerous options here. Some portfolios are obvious no-nos. They may be cheap and workmanlike but they don't create a good impression. You have various options based on the basic black loose-leafed portfolio case. These range in price according to quality and size. And yes, size matters.

The no-nos include the kind of folder with clear plastic pockets that you can buy in a stationery store. They're all right for storing loose student work, but are best avoided at professional level. This applies equally to concertina document files, which also fall into the 'stationery' category.

The same largely goes for the card-backed portfolios with string ties that are designed more for holding artists' drawings. Everything in them is loose; there are strings to tie and untie and flaps to deal with. They are simply not very practical in portfolio meetings.

Then there are several variations on a theme, based on the simple black portfolio with replaceable sleeves. The bottom end of this range is the Artcare black vinyl (or woven nylon) zip-up case with four- or five-ring binders that hold quite sturdy plastic sleeves, which generally come with black cover-paper inserts. Sizes range from A4 (297 x 210mm/11.7 x 8.3in) to the rather unwieldy A1 (841 x 594mm/33.1 x 23.4in). This is really the starter range, but the cases are very practical. Given how much wear and tear a portfolio may suffer while being couriered around by bike, they can withstand a fair amount of rough handling.

The middle range of this kind of portfolio is made by a French company, Panodia. The cases have multiple-ring binders that run the length of the spine, thereby giving the sleeves more support, and making them less prone to torn eyelets. The sleeves for these portfolios are also made from a lighter, finer quality of acetate. The outside cases are available in vinyl or leather, but both are zipped to protect the contents. I have used these and found that they do improve the overall feel and quality of presentation, but the sleeves tend to scuff when they rub against one another, so they wear more quickly. Given that portfolios get handled a lot, keeping an eye on this kind of thing is part of the general maintenance and upkeep of your folio, along with refreshing its contents.

The next level of portfolio within this 'standard black' category is the leather binder that is designed to have its own carrying case, so no zip-up sides. It is double the cost of the mid-range zip-up portfolios. Photographers tend to favour these folios. They can be embossed with your name or a logo or graphic of some description, and are thereby personalized, as well as looking more professional. The one problem is that these portfolios don't seem to come with a corresponding bag or case to fit. The sleeves are made from good-quality acetate, with black cover-paper inserts, and the binding system consists of four brass screws. These cases look businesslike and give off an air of quality.

Within the above categories, most notably the Artcare range, some are available in different colours. I've seen all the above for sale in specialist outlets in New York, so they are very probably available in North America generally as well as in Europe. If you live in a different part of the world, there are likely to be local equivalents, if not the exact same brands. In terms of cost and quality, the cases described largely cover your presentation options.

Along with colours other than black, there is potential for a more idiosyncratic approach to portfolios. You can create your own portfolio and carrying case, fully personalized with your own drawings or graphics. These can certainly stand out in a big 'portfolio call' (where an agency calls in lots of portfolios for a potential campaign), but ultimately it's the work inside that needs to do the talking.

Whichever approach you go for, your portfolio needs to be well thought-out, with the choice of work carefully considered, and, of course, it needs to be well presented.

Tailoring the portfolio to the client: pros and cons

> Some illustrators structure their portfolio (or portfolios) according to different stylistic approaches, which can be tailored to specific client types. There may have been a time when having such a range of styles would have been considered an asset. If you really do have two very distinct approaches that are original and equally developed and consistent, then there might be an argument for this. However, I would suggest that nowadays you need to focus your efforts on one approach, not dissipate them by having an alternative. In the highly competitive environment that exists these days, why use someone who does a little bit of cross-hatched line work, or a bit of fashion-style drawing, when you can get a swathe of people who do nothing but such work? I would say that people commissioning illustrators do so knowing what kind of feel they want on the page. It's as unique as a designer's choice of typeface, and I suspect that, if they were faced with a range of work in one portfolio, they might worry about which particular style would end up appearing on their page.

However, some benefit remains in having a portfolio flexible enough to be tailored to specific requirements. If a company calls in your portfolio for a particular job, it is generally useful to show material that reflects what a client has said they are looking for. It might not be a favourite piece of work or, under normal circumstances, something you would bother to include, but it could tip the balance in your favour when it comes to choosing which illustrator gets the job.

The clients most likely to appreciate a tailored portfolio — say, one featuring lots of examples of animals, if that is what they are looking for — are advertising agencies. A great many ad agencies aren't that interested in the conceptual content of an illustrator's work. What they are after is a look and feel for the image they need rendered. Because they are so heavily involved in marketing, and will ultimately be thinking about 'take up' rates for whatever product or service they are advertising, the idea component will have been carefully thought through and presented to the client before they choose how it's going to look.

Because there are a great number of people involved in the approval process for advertising campaigns, agencies can't go through potentially tortuous meetings

Luke Hayman

Partner, Pentagram New York

When do you call on the services of illustration?
> I'm currently a partner at Pentagram, a multidisciplinary design firm. We've used illustration for so many reasons: when photography isn't available, or when a conceptual image is required, or for branding a section of a magazine, or when a lack of specificity is required, or for texture and pacing, or for cost …

Where do you find talent?
> Mostly from the internet or seeing work; occasionally from cold calls and recommendations.

How do you feel about cropping and adjusting artwork?
> It should be done in consultation with the illustrator. If more work is needed beyond the initial brief, then more money should be paid. There are usually good reasons for changes; it shouldn't be arbitrary.

Do you ever reject artwork?
> We've rejected portraits where likenesses were poor. We've also rejected work that didn't live up to our expectations. Occasionally an artist has a few great pieces in their portfolio but has trouble reaching that level consistently.

What kind of promotional items work best for you?
> Postcards or small booklets are best. Mailings that seem generic and inappropriate for the magazine are ineffective. Memorable items include a 'bobble-head' of the illustrator, a 50 x 70mm (2 x 3in) hardbound book, and a newsletter with original editorial content.

John Maeda for *I.D.* magazine, (photo originally shot by Graham MacIndoe). Design, Luke Hayman

Do you see many portfolios? If so, what criteria do you use when choosing who to see?
> To be honest, I rarely see illustrators with portfolios. Perhaps if they are young, new, from out of town, recommended by a colleague and have lots of talent, or sometimes through personal recommendation or someone whose work I've noticed and have been interested in. Very occasionally it will be an unsolicited e-mail where the work seems particularly original so we'll make the time.

What do you look for in them?
> Just great work – ideas, execution and originality.

Since you can see work on screen, what would you ideally like to see in a portfolio these days? An aide memoire to what they do, or something extra?
> Extra is better – even through the presentation of the portfolio itself. It's easy to bring an iPad or laptop and click through the site but it doesn't have the impact and is often a little disappointing. The iPad is great for animations.

Given the ease of viewing images online, do you still feel inclined to see artists with their portfolios?
> When there's time it's nice to meet the person and to see the work in a physical form. Sometimes artists bring books or large-scale prints that make the work more special through use of materials and colours that don't translate to the screen.

What do you think of illustrators' websites?
> They are very useful – they're the equivalent of calling in a portfolio. But we go to a site to see work: an experimental site can be fine as long as it doesn't

get in the way. Speed, simplicity and large images work best; common irritants are slowness, confusing navigation and intro screens or sequences.

Do you source artists via social media?

> Only friends who happen to be illustrators. I don't 'follow' artists.

What's your view on the promotional value of social media sites? Their pros and cons?

> I am not a power user of social media. I haven't worked out how to separate the personal stuff from the professional very well … I typically search for the artist's name and find their website. Sometimes it's interesting to click through an artist's blog.

How do you feel about working via an agent?

> Working with a rep to solicit the work and to negotiate a fee is good, but sometimes – especially when talking about work – the agent feels like an unnecessary middle man (or woman). You can be deprived of the nuances of the to and fro of a conversation.

What are the benefits for you?

> A rep can serve as a manager of an illustrator's time. They let you know if the artist is away from their desk, or at the beach for two weeks, or overbooked and so on. It's also easier to have a good relationship with a single agent who can mediate between you and all of their artists.

How do you feel about contracts taking copyright?

> I have no problem provided an appropriate fee is negotiated.

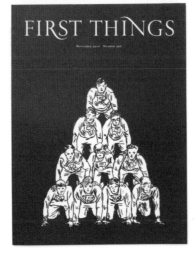

You should resist signing if you feel you are being taken advantage of.

What do you like most about working with illustrators?

> I love collaboration, particularly when an idea is improved, and being involved with smart and beautiful image-making.

What would prevent you recommissioning?

Cover designs for *First Things* magazine by Luke Hayman and Shigeto Akiyama, with illustrations by Leanne Shapton

> A negative attitude; inflexibility.

What would be your one 'do'?

> Be thoughtful.

What would be your 'don't'?

> Don't take things personally.

to get an idea approved only for the illustrator to go away and reinterpret the brief. However, I'm aware, as I write this, that things are changing, and that the more adventurous agencies are looking for illustrators who can bring a more pronounced creative input to campaigns. For them, it isn't only about the look and feel, but the illustrator's attitude, wit and visual agility. So, you need to heed the above and, of course, totally ignore it.

'I can count on one hand the number of times I've been asked for a paper portfolio. As far as editorial work is concerned, I think for a lot of art directors, seeing work online is enough to get a feel for what a person does.'

Sam Weber, Illustrator

Going back to the selection process for your portfolio, it might be that, in having so much work to choose from, you leave out pieces that are too similar and thus risk appearing repetitive. These may well come to the fore, however, if your portfolio is called in specifically for that kind of work, and you can then compose it predominantly along such lines.

The other argument for flexibility is that not all work is suitable for all clients. As an illustrator, you could end up working for a broad range of clients. Having a portfolio that shows this range in your work may be appropriate for, say, 75 per cent of your clients, but there may be 25 per cent for whom only certain types of image are relevant. Having one flexible, changeable portfolio is one option; however, if there is a specific split in your client base, then perhaps it's sufficient to justify a second portfolio containing a wholly different mix of work.

Personally, I don't favour this kind of approach, but some swear by it. I feel that the range of work you choose should show the breadth of your approach, thinking and conceptualizing, and that a designer or art director should be able to judge your suitability on that basis. Some clients, most notably advertising agencies, need to see the cats in your portfolio if they are looking for someone to draw a cat for a campaign. It's a cliché but it holds true, as it is partly how advertising agencies work. In such a situation, some might argue that a portfolio of nothing but cats drawn in different styles would undoubtedly get the job. I might add a couple of different pieces to the portfolio if I thought that their inclusion would be appropriate, but I wouldn't tailor an entire folio in order to meet a specific client's needs.

Digital portfolios > A digital portfolio allows for a great deal of flexibility in presentation, choice of images and any shuffling or changing of images you might wish to do. A PDF of a selection of images can be a reasonably small file to e-mail (if the recipient is happy to receive samples in that way) or burn to a disk and post. There are many simple 'slide show' applications that allow you to drop images into a file that, when opened, displays the images in a set order, with a fade between each one. Preparing items to send to people, which is more about promotion than a portfolio, is particularly easy when done digitally.

If you are going to send items prepared as a presentation, try to choose a common software application or file-sharing site from which a link can be e-mailed. There should be zero hassle for the client, which ultimately works in your favour too. Try to resist getting too clever. What people want to see is great work, not an impressive method of display, particularly if viewing the impressive display entails such extra work for the recipient as downloading software he or she doesn't already have. If someone has asked you to send some examples of your work, check how they would like to receive them. If in doubt, use the simplest option.

A digital portfolio is undoubtedly flexible, but you need to consider how convenient it is for someone to view at, for example, a face-to-face meeting. Most people still prefer to flick through a 'book' portfolio, to see what images look like on a page, rather than at screen resolution. I'd say that a digital portfolio is handy to support your 'book' version, but should not replace it. If you have a website, it's effectively your digital portfolio anyway; and if someone can view that, without you being there, why would they bother to have a meeting where you show them something similar on disk or your own laptop or iPad brought along for the purpose?

Choosing your own solution

> A good portfolio is the key to a successful presentation. In a meeting you generally have one chance to create an impression. Get it wrong, and you'll struggle thereafter to keep the client interested. It's worth spending time and some money to get it right. Illustration, like most businesses these days, is highly competitive.

It's difficult for anyone to advise someone blindly on how they should put a portfolio together when there are so many different kinds of illustration out there. Much is ultimately dictated by the nature of the work, whether there are manageable originals to show, the consistency of quality, general stylistic approach and the quantity of work that is worth showing to any would-be commissioners. The advice here is designed to provoke some thought as to how you present your work. Each case is, in the end, unique. Also, you will always present it better the second, third and fourth time, and so on. You learn with experience, and much of it comes down to gut instinct, which can't be taught. Part of leaving college is about realizing that teaching exposes you to multiple educated opinions. All are valuable but, in the end, you have to make your own decisions and accept that you made the best one you could at the time. There will be some you regret, but learn from your mistakes. Nobody is perfect.

Bruce Ingman

Can you provide a brief outline of your studies?

> I studied for a BA in Fine Art at Nottingham Trent Polytechnic and an MA in Illustration at the Royal College of Art.

How well did your studies prepare you for working as an illustrator?

> At Nottingham I had a friend who ran the film society and he asked me to do the posters. I liked the discipline of a deadline, having to make swift decisions and finish things quickly, something I rarely did in the studio. I would silkscreen the posters at the weekend and then put them up around the college on the Monday. It felt like I had this great big art gallery. I really enjoyed having this mixed audience for my work rather than just my friends and tutors. When I got to the RCA it was run on a similar basis: they gave you a studio and you just got on with your self-directed projects. What was great about the RCA was that a lot of my fellow students were very dedicated to being illustrators and you learned a lot from being around them as well as from the tutors.

What were your first experiences of working as an illustrator?

> When I left college I was very unsure as to what direction I wanted to take. I just sat in my studio and painted. I'd had quite a bit of commissioned work by that stage, from newspapers and magazines, but I wasn't too sure if that was the route I wanted to go down, being a jobbing illustrator. I went to see lots of design agencies. I enjoyed going to meet people, seeing where they worked and what they were like. You soon found out if you could work with them or not.

Any memorable incidents from this period?

> How unadventurous quite a lot of art directors seemed to be. They usually wanted something exactly like they'd seen in your portfolio. But what gave one hope was coming across really enlightened art directors. I was lucky; I went to visit *The Observer Magazine* quite early on and met Cath Caldwell and Martin Colyer, who commissioned me straight away. I asked if they knew of anyone else I could see with my portfolio and Cath wrote me a long list, which opened quite a few doors. There would be times when work would start to dry up and that's another good reason to have a studio – if you are lucky, your studio colleagues would support you. They would give you tips on who to go and see.

How did you cope financially?

> Barely. But all I ever wanted to do was to paint so I just worked as hard as I could. My wife reminded me the other day that when I first went to see her (she was an editor in a publishing house) the lining of my coat was stuck together with masking tape to stop it falling apart.

Are you methodical in your working life?

> I have become more methodical in terms of knowing how I work best. But I wouldn't ever want it to become too routine. I will always push a deadline. I think it comes from working for art directors who push for delivery and then sit on the artwork for ages before sending it to repro.

Do you work from home or a studio?

> I got a studio pretty much as soon as I left college. I think you need a place to go to in the morning and interact with people otherwise you become myopic.

Do you have an agent/rep?

> I've had agents, and there are good and bad points to having one. The main bad one, obviously, is that they can take 30 per cent of your fee. A lot of them have too many illustrators on their books. The benefits are that you can get on with doing what you do best while they are getting you more work. They will hopefully know how to negotiate better, or at least fairer, fees. Also, it's good to have a sounding board. However, I feel I've established good relationships in publishing, so I like dealing with publishers directly.

Do you use social media?

> I've finally succumbed, and so far so good. It provides an amazing amount of support and enthusiasm among the illustrator community. You no longer need to feel isolated. We could almost be in a vast open-plan studio!

Is social media important in promoting your work? Do you see a return?

> Yes, it has become naturally

Illustrators: Bruce Ingman

43

integrated into the routine. It can only be positive to be less reliant on the publisher to promote your work. It was a hard lesson to learn that publishers can't sell all their books, all at the same time. Yes, people have been in contact for work. And you make vital connections with clients, schools and bookshops. Of course, most importantly, it enables you to work more closely and successfully with your publisher.

Do you have a website?

> Yes. Some kind of presence on the net is essential. I do quite a lot of literary festivals, school visits etc. and it's good for people to get in contact. It brings you closer to the readers. Apart from its usefulness, I think we have to embrace the online community or get left behind.

Has the promotional landscape changed in the last six years?

> Completely. Facebook, Twitter, blogs have completely reshaped the landscape. Everyone has a virtual voice.

Do you see clients face to face?

> Yes. I like meeting people, so from time to time I'll go and see someone. Also, sometimes I'm contacted by people and I'll have a meeting with them, look them in the eye! I think meeting a client face to face is really important. I got a commission from a US publisher initially via an e-mail contact and, even though we had a good working relationship via e-mail and phone, I wish I'd got on a plane and met them at the beginning of the project. I met them afterwards and they were great. I think you can tell once you've met someone if you can trust them.

Have you had any bad experiences with clients?

> Yes, in the early days, doing work for people and then not getting paid, the usual stuff. And for all the means of contact at our disposal, the simple act of returning a phone call can still cause problems.

Have you ever turned work down for reasons other than not being available?

> I have turned down quite a few stories, although nothing I've regretted. If your heart isn't going to be in it, you shouldn't do it. It will show and could be detrimental to your reputation.

What do you like most about being an illustrator?

> Doing something I love and getting paid to do it. Being able to walk into a bookshop, school, library, in New York, Paris, Tokyo, and see a copy of my book. Illustrating stories by writers you really admire. As a children's book author/illustrator, being part of someone's memory of childhood. What is more special than that?

What do you like least?

> Poor vision from so-called creative people. Graphic designers doing derivative Photoshop artwork instead of commissioning original artwork.

What do you think is the future of illustration?

> While such traditional areas as editorial are shrinking, there are new areas opening up globally. I think more self-publishing is already happening and will become the norm. On the positive side, graphic novels might finally be establishing themselves as a force. But I think (and hope) there's still life in the picture book.

Offer one piece of advice to a new illustrator.

> Be honest, be intuitive, work really hard and don't give up. Don't wait to be commissioned, initiate your own projects. And if you meet someone who likes your work, get them to give you a contact of someone else who they think would like your work.

"Funny, touching, ridiculous and dramatic – a treat from start to finish." *Guardian*

THE RUNAWAY DINNER

Allan Ahlberg • Bruce Ingman

Well then, of course, as you might expect,
the fork ran after the sausage,
the knife ran after the fork,
the plate ran after the knife,
the little table and the little chair ran after the plate,

and Banjo, that hungry little boy, ran after all of them.

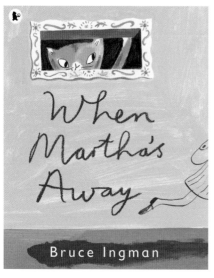

This page: Cover and pages from *The Pencil*

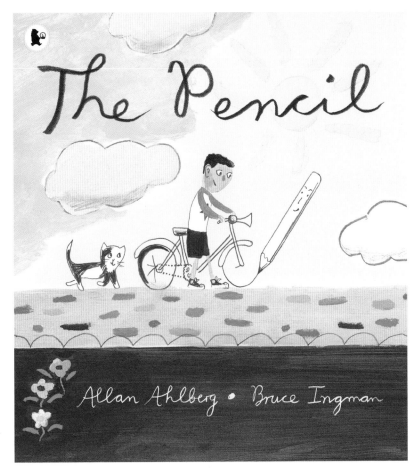

Chapter 3
Job-hunting and interviews

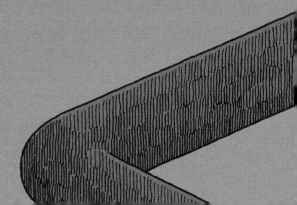

**You and your portfolio
are ready ...**

> You are now ready to pick up the phone to make appointments and start showing your portfolio to would-be clients. An accepted 'model career path', although not one you need necessarily follow, is that new illustrators begin by doing editorial work. Publishing, design and advertising jobs tend to come after some exposure within this field. That said, there are plenty of cases where people are snapped up by advertising clients first, then have to look for editorial work after that. Similarly, some people's work lends itself more immediately to the world of book publishing. You should consider seeing all of the categories of potential client, but there is a practical reason underpinning that 'model career path'.

Frequent and regular commissioners of illustration are to be found at magazines and newspapers, in the sector defined as 'editorial'. The simple reason for this is that they have regular, repetitive print deadlines, with publications containing material that needs to be illustrated. If magazines are monthly, they'll be commissioning every month; if they are weekly, they'll be looking for illustrations every week. Newspapers will be either daily or weekly, depending on the section or issue of the newspaper. This means there are many more opportunities to be commissioned in the editorial arena than in any other.

*'Some illustrators who
contact us seem never
to have looked at the
newspaper, which
is always irritating.
We are most likely to
commission people who
do the kind of work we
can use; anything else
is a waste of their time
and ours.'*

Mark Porter, former
Creative Director,
The Guardian

This, in turn, means that you gain experience in answering briefs, which you can then demonstrate to clients in publishing and design. Advertising briefs operate in a different way, but this will be covered later in the chapter. Book publishers have semi-frequent commissioning, with correspondingly longer deadlines. The jobs tend to be book covers, although occasionally books also require small internal illustrations.

Design companies deal with 'brand creation' (i.e. logos, 'identities' and their application), business-to-business communications, annual reports, packaging and so on. Some may have a particular area of expertise, such as a strong packaging portfolio, or annual reports and company brochures. Design companies may also deal with cultural projects, such as exhibition or concert posters, or charitable events. While some may have a reputation as fans of illustration, using it whenever they can, in general they tend to have an irregular, if not infrequent, need for it. Any illustration they propose to a client may be accompanied by a choice of approaches, as well as a photographic option. So, when they want to commission illustration, there is always the chance that the client would prefer, if not the photographic route, perhaps the alternative illustration that was put forward alongside your work. Consequently, compared to an editorial situation, there are fewer opportunities to be commissioned and relatively more chances not to be chosen because there are more people involved in the choice of illustration. This isn't intended to put you off approaching design clients, but rather to give you a practical understanding of how things work, and to reiterate why editorial work is such a good starting point for an illustrator's career.

Advertising is a whirlwind of highs and lows and potential jobs that simply don't happen. You need to learn not to get too excited until a job is definitely happening.

Partly because of the huge amount of money involved in advertising (which doesn't even take into account any fees paid to an illustrator), there are more decision-makers involved, more options proposed to the client and, correspondingly, more opportunities for the client to choose a different route and for the job to go to someone else. That said, advertising agencies are voracious consumers of new talent and ideas, always on the lookout for something fresh and previously unseen that might be an indicator of an up-and-coming trend. Because their briefs tend to be a lot more prescriptive, they are often more interested in style than ideas, and may prefer to tell you what to draw. You may well be asked to create their idea in your 'handwriting', rather than offer your own ideas. There are, however, refreshing exceptions to this, where an art director recognizes what an illustrator can contribute, and gives general guidance on what the agency is trying to achieve, leaving the illustrator to inject his or her own magic into a project.

So, as a young would-be illustrator, you need to land your first job, and get some money flowing into your bank account. The obvious place to start is where the work is in abundance and the risks for someone commissioning a novice illustrator are reduced. It makes sense, then, to start looking in editorial departments. As already mentioned, it's not a career path set in stone, so try to see people from all the various sectors. You might just strike lucky.

Editorial clients   **>** How do you decide who to see in editorial departments? There will be the usual suspects – regular commissioners of the illustrations that appear frequently in national newspapers and consumer magazines. But remember that there are also many publications that don't appear so readily in the public domain; these are the contract publishing titles and trade magazines, or subscription-only titles.

Doing some basic research simply entails going to any reasonably sized newsagent, where you can browse the magazines without the proprietor of the shop getting tetchy about you thumbing through them. You can start with those whose subjects interest you, but you really need to look out for ones that use illustration. Narrow these down to the magazines that use illustrations you like, or that you can see your work sitting alongside. This will usually give you a good indication of the kind of eye for illustration that the art director or commissioner at the magazine has.

The essential information about who to see at that publication can, within limits, be found in the magazine itself. There is a page, usually at the front (or occasionally at the back), that lists the key staff, from the editor down. It should also give the address of the publication and the main switchboard number.

To find out who commissions illustration at a particular magazine, first look for the design director, art director or art editor. A design director may manage the design team, rather than commissioning directly, but getting his or her interest may well prove influential with other designers on the magazine, so it's worth having your work seen by him or her if possible. The art director or art editor can sometimes be in a similar position, in that he or she manages a team of designers who commission, rather than micro-managing every illustration-commissioning decision. On a magazine, there may well be other designers responsible for the different sections. They may not be listed individually, but they will nevertheless be in a position to commission illustration for each issue. Further research will be needed to identify them. Ask around among friends who are illustrators or designers, or try asking any contacts you make. It is worth phoning the magazine's main switchboard and seeing if the receptionist can tell you who works in the art department alongside the named art director. Ask for the name of the art editor, for example, or the senior designer.

The approval process for selecting an illustrator will vary from magazine to magazine. Some decisions are editor-led; others need the approval of the senior designer, be it the art director or art editor, who may delegate this kind of decision to the individual designers on different sections of the magazine. This, in turn, mirrors the approval process for roughs or sketch-stage work.

You now have the title of a magazine that carries illustration you think suits your approach, the name of the art director or art editor, and the address and telephone number – in short, the information you need in order to try to get an appointment to see the person commissioning on that title. To fill in the blanks in your information, you need to make the most of any meeting you manage to have. This applies to all the various types of client, though, not just editorial clients – I'll come to this a little later on.

Publishing clients > As in the case of editorial clients, there are the 'usual suspects' – the key publishing houses – and then there are plenty of less well-known publishers who also commission illustration. The budget available is likely to reflect the size of the publishing house, but they are all potential commissioners. Many of what you might think of as smaller or less well-known publishers are in fact subsidiaries or imprints of the larger ones. An obvious example would be Random House, which consists of its main imprint plus Knopf, Vintage, Arrow, Doubleday, Jonathan Cape and many others. The same holds true for the likes of HarperCollins and Penguin. As with magazines, begin by doing some research in bookshops.

Browse for books with exciting covers that interest you. Many of the covers will be one-offs for a particular author, perhaps for a new novel. However, look out for complete backlists of well-known authors that might have been recently re-released with a series of new covers (either all by the same illustrator or a bunch of different ones). This is often a good indicator of whether a publishing house has a sympathetic view of illustration. This often changes with market trends, but since so many publishers, particularly the big houses, are nowadays answerable (if not beholden) to their sales and marketing departments, the fact that they are re-releasing a backlist with new illustrations, or pushing new releases with illustrated covers, generally indicates that they see illustration as an important sales tool for their books (and that their marketing department agrees with them).

Finding out who to see is a lot less straightforward. If you are lucky, there will be a design credit alongside the illustration credit, and that will give you the name of someone to try to contact. The publisher's address and telephone number should be easy enough to find on the imprint page, which details the date of publication, ISBN and so on. Failing that, resort to the phone book or directory enquiries.

At the large publishing houses, there are many designers dealing with the various different imprints. Each imprint may have several individuals working on the covers of its books, particularly if the list is sizeable. The designer will generally commission the cover artwork. There may be a chain of command that requires approval by a superior, but the designer responsible for a particular book's jacket will choose or propose a cover artist (or photographer).

A series of books for Spanish publisher Losada with illustrations by Marion Deuchars. Cover design by Fernando Gutierrez

As mentioned above, it's unlikely that you will get the designer's name from the information in the book as it's not standard practice to credit him or her (although it does happen occasionally). You can try calling the publishing house and asking for the art department, then explaining why you are calling to whoever answers. You could use a couple of different approaches, saying that you were hoping to see someone with your portfolio, or that you would like to know who you should send samples of your work to. Always ask whether there is more than one person who might be interested in receiving them. It's unlikely you'll get in to meet a publishing designer without them first seeing some samples and deciding they want to see more, or without being recommended by someone they know.

Unless they want you to come in specifically for a briefing, many publishers have a strict 'drop off' policy, where you are expected to drop off your portfolio on a designated day and pick it up 24 or 48 hours later. It's the most practical way for them to handle all the potential illustrators and photographers who want to show their portfolios.

Design clients > Unlike the editorial and publishing sectors, there is less direct access to information about who designs what in the design sector. Many items that might appear in the public arena, such as packaging, will not have a credit detailing who designed it. Things like annual reports may well carry design credits, but you're unlikely to get hold of an annual report unless you're a shareholder in the company. However, designers do like to get their work noticed, this being an important means of attracting new clients. To this end, they try to get their work into such industry magazines as *Creative Review*, *Design Week* and *i-D*, or enter it in competitions such as the Design & Art Direction Awards (D&AD) or the Society of Publication Designers Awards. Keeping up with the trade

Simon Esterson

Principal, Esterson Associates

Can you briefly outline your current role?
> The studio designs, launches and redesigns magazines and newspapers.

What was your first experience of working with an illustrator?
> I asked Peter Till to do a black-and-white magazine cover 30 years ago. I still work with Peter.

Did you have a mentor who introduced you to illustration?
> I was influenced by the work of Michael Rand at *The Sunday Times Magazine* and David Driver at the *Radio Times*. I worked with Mike Lackersteen and Martin Colyer and learned how to make it happen.

What is your general opinion of illustration as an allied creative discipline?
> I can't draw so I'm in awe of anybody who can.

Why and when do you call on its services?
> When it's a complex idea that needs simple explanation. When you've already got too many photographs. When the article makes you laugh. When you've just seen a great piece of work and think, 'I must get that illustrator to do something …'

Do you keep a stable of illustrators who you turn to frequently?
> Yes, although more a repertory cast than a stable.

Are there examples you feel show illustration at its best?
> I've worked on reportage illustration projects with Paul Cox, Lucinda Rogers and Matthew Cook. I enjoyed those because

you actually send people to places.

How do you find working with them as creative individuals?
> I love the moment of opening the envelope containing finished artwork. Now it's opening a file, but I get the same pleasure.

Are there promotional activities you feel don't work?
> Those big books now feel out of tune with the times, creatively and environmentally.

How do you decide whether to see someone with their portfolio?
> Does their work fit the kind of things we do? I will often look online first, but I do like to meet people and talk.

What is your experience of illustrators' websites?
> I think the web is an amazing thing for illustrators and photographers. I can look at work at any time of the day by anybody anywhere in the world.

What do you think works well?
> Telling people what the work is and who it was for.

Are there common irritants?
> As for any site, bad navigation.

What do you feel about working through an agent?
> For an agent, fees are often a problem with editorial illustration. But there can be logistical benefits. If it smooths the process, great. If it gets in the way, not so great.

What do you feel about fees?
> Of course they're not high enough. I'm happy to negotiate if illustrators feel they are too low.

What do you like most about working with illustrators?
> As with any creative relationship, the excitement of watching somebody else doing something better than you thought possible.

What would prevent you recommissioning?
> A great rough, followed by bad art.

What would be your advice to a new, would-be illustrator?
> Find your voice, not somebody else's.

Given the ease of viewing images online, do you still feel inclined to see artists?
> Yes. It's more about meeting them, hearing them talking about their work, than seeing the portfolio. I think it can lead to a better working relationship. But it's not vital: one of the excitements of digital working is being able to collaborate with anybody, anywhere. I read artists' blogs, follow their links.

Illustrations by Laura
Carlin for Candrian
Catering brochure

press will keep you informed of what's going on in graphic design. In addition, most industry magazines carry sections showcasing recent work by design companies, either as a round-up of interesting projects, or as a feature on a particular designer or company. Trawling through these magazines should yield the names of those design companies that make extensive use of illustration, or that simply seem to be doing innovative work. In most cases you will find the designer will be credited or mentioned in the accompanying copy.

Alternatively, try to get hold of awards books, which showcase work that includes illustration. These should provide the names of the designers as well as the companies responsible.

Another way to find out who is doing what in design is to check out publications like *Adweek* or *Campaign*. These will tell you, on a more 'newsy', gossipy basis, who has won particular accounts with certain clients. You may already have seen the work out and about; now you know who designed it.

Advertising clients > Advertising companies vary in size, calibre of work and their need for illustration services. In common with any market sector, there are the obvious major players, which, in the case of advertising, would be Ogilvy & Mather, BBDO, Weiden+Kennedy, McCann-Erickson and BBH (Bartle Bogle Hegarty), most of which have an international presence. As with design companies, the best way to find out who is doing what, and who is using illustration to do it, is by looking through the creative press and advertising trade press, such as *Campaign* and *Print* magazines. Both *Print* and *Communication Arts* have annual awards and 'round-up' editions that showcase the best of the previous year. As they tend to list the art directors as well as the design and advertising companies involved, they are a mine of information and can help to pinpoint who particularly likes illustration at a given company.

If you approach an advertising company, your first point of contact will probably be its art buyer. Most agencies will have more than one, but there will be a senior buyer who manages the others. I understand the buyer's role as that of creative hub for the agency; they are the people who buy in the creative services that an art director needs to realize the vision for a campaign, including illustration. Art buyers should know what is going on out in the wider creative community, and what is available when art directors ask for a particular style or feel of work.

The advertising campaign process runs something like this. A creative team consisting of an art director and copywriter is given the brief for a client's campaign. The team then comes up with ideas for images for the campaign and snappy copy to accompany the visuals. The art director will have an idea of how he or she wants the images to look, and the team will look for the person who can execute them in the style they want. They may be well tuned in to who is doing what, and they may know who they would like to do the campaign. If so, they will ask the art buyer to get that person's portfolio in. Alternatively, they will describe what they want and the buyer may then look at a range of people who could produce the results the team would like to achieve. The buyer will then call an agent, explain what the company is looking for and ask for any suitable portfolios to be sent in to the creative team, or request portfolios from one or two specific illustrators. Buyers may also trawl through the various illustration books that are available, or through their own files of samples, and then call individual illustrators and ask them to send in their portfolios.

The point at which they involve an illustrator depends on the agency's approval process. An art buyer may approach you with a request for a 'pitch artwork', where you are briefed to produce an image or images that will convey to a client what the campaign would look like if it were to go ahead. Depending on individual scenarios, it might be black-and-white sketches, a rough, semi-finished colour artwork or even a fully rendered artwork – whatever is needed to convince the client to give the go-ahead on that approach to the campaign.

With pitch artworks, there is an understanding that they are for client presentation only. A nominal fee may be offered for something less than a full artwork; in the case of a full artwork, a fee is negotiated that reflects the work involved in creating it. There are various factors involved, and we will look at fee negotiation in Chapter 4. There is also a chance that you will be asked to do a pitch artwork for free. I generally say no to this: something, however nominal, should be paid for your time. It's a point of principle and good faith, even if the fee agreed does not reflect the work involved.

You may bypass this stage if it has already been reached using the art director's scribbled sketches or an agency's in-house visualizer. If so, your portfolio will be presented, and whether or not you are selected to execute the campaign will come down to a matter of agency and client preference. If you are selected, the art buyer will negotiate the appropriate fees with you for the artworking part of the job and for any media licences the agency may wish to purchase. The buyer liaises between the art director, client, client account handler/executive, and you.

Most agents have very good relations with many art buyers, established over time and by working together on projects, so that each understands how the other operates. Ideally, this leads to everyone striving for a win–win outcome to negotiations, with no party left feeling disgruntled as a result of being overcharged or underpaid.

While illustration agencies appreciate these good working relationships, it's also important to understand that the ideal way of getting involved

Jason Ford billboards for American Airlines

in an ad campaign is for an art director to have you and your work in mind before they even know what form the campaign will take. Your work then becomes integral to the campaign, rather than a cosmetic coating of style. Both approaches can work, but given a preference, I would always choose to play an integral role. There's a greater chance that the commission will proceed smoothly, and it also increases your chances of eventually getting the job.

Getting your work in front of the relevant art directors, then, is obviously crucial, but identifying them can be difficult. One route is to get to know the art buyer and learn from him or her which art directors really like illustration. You can then send samples or links to your website directly to them. Some buyers are quite guarded about the art directors they work with and want everything to go to them in the first instance. If that is the case, respect this and don't push them for information, as you'll only make yourself unpopular; ultimately you need to

Phil Hankinson's
billboard for Vodafone
(philhankinson.com)

maintain good relations with art buyers. That said, it doesn't mean you can't get your information from other sources and then approach the names you've found. Again, awards annuals and the creative press are good starting points. While you can buy lists of advertising creatives, they are unlikely to tell you which individuals commission illustration, or even like it. Given that there are lots of creatives at an advertising agency, you will be shooting blind this way, while the information you glean from the creative press or awards annuals will include what these individuals have actually done.

Buying lists **>** An alternative means of getting to know who is commissioning illustration is to buy a list. There are several companies, including File FX and Workbook, that sell database lists for the various sectors: advertising, design, magazines, book publishing and so on. It's a direct way to get information on all the commissioning areas. These companies also produce lists for major cities, as well as ones with nationwide coverage. You can therefore pick and choose who to target, and how much to spend. It's always worth checking when a list was last updated and when it is next due to be revised, so that you can buy information that is as fresh as possible. Bear in mind that you will have to update your purchased lists yourself, either by making calls to verify that the information is still correct, or by buying new versions from the list seller later on.

In the US, there is a great online list or database service called Agency Access. It's more expensive than buying a printed list piecemeal, but you get a vast amount of information that is regularly updated. You can search by company name, or by individual if you are trying to locate an art director who has moved on; you can also select by companies that use illustration frequently, occasionally, rarely or never. It lists the accounts they work on and their annual turnover, so you can see what kind of organization you're pitching to. Although more expensive, Agency Access has various payment options to allow you to spread the cost over the year. At the outset it may not be an expense you want to incur, but once you get rolling I'd say it's a good investment.

There are other online databases, including BikiniLists, which covers the US, UK and Europe. Again, check the frequency of updates when you subscribe. Some databases are revised monthly, some quarterly. Wherever you get your information from, you need to ensure that you collate it in a usable form and update it regularly; designers tend to move around rather a lot.

The big meeting ...   **>** It's impossible to predict or dictate how any meeting might go, but here are some general principles that you might find helpful. The points should hold true for a meeting with anyone from any of the different sectors discussed.

Once you manage to get an appointment, ensure that you are there on time. It might sound rather obvious, but nobody wants to have a scheduled meeting happen 10, 15 or 20 minutes later than intended. Unforeseen delays can occur, but few people are interested in hearing that the bus was late or that the walk from the tube took longer than you thought. If in doubt, leave extra time for your journey. It's better to be ten minutes early, sitting in reception, than ten minutes late for someone who is making time to see you. After all, you want them on your side, not irritated with you from the outset. If a genuine delay occurs, call the client, tell them you've been delayed and that you anticipate being 10 or 15 minutes late, and ask them if that is still okay for them. Don't assume that it will be simply because it is okay for you. They may have another appointment, or may only have had that particular window in which to see you. If you call in advance and warn them you are running late, you give them the opportunity to reschedule or cancel. So, make sure you leave plenty of travelling time, keep your mobile charged and have the client's phone number on you. Even if you end up getting voicemail, you've done your best to forewarn them, which will be appreciated and should prevent the meeting getting off to a poor start.

Do you still see artists with their portfolios? 'Definitely. I really love meeting the artists, I really like hearing information about the work that only the artist can tell you. It's interesting and useful for me.'

Sarah Thomson,
Art Buyer

When you go to see a prospective client, try to see as many people as possible. The designer or art director who has agreed to see you and your portfolio may go through the book with you fairly quickly, limit the meeting to just the two of you, take your samples and that will be it: in and out, short and sweet.

However, most designers who are prepared to see you and your portfolio are enthusiasts and are generally interested in getting the measure of you. If appropriate – and this will vary from company to company and situation to situation – they may well call over colleagues so that the book is viewed by several people simultaneously. If they work for a company that publishes several titles, they may take you to see the designer or art director on a different publication. Some like to share, some like to guard their 'sources' and – jealously – keep you to themselves. Try asking whether they think any of their colleagues might be able to look at the portfolio while you are there. They'll respond either positively or not, so don't force the issue; but it's always worth asking.

If you are introduced to several people while showing your book, try to get their business cards or note their names. Carry a small notebook and tell them you'd like to write down their names so you don't forget who you've been talking to. You'll look prepared, and if you are open about why you've taken a notebook out, you're less likely to get flustered. If the response to your work is enthusiastic and they like the samples, promise to send them updates from time to time.

When it comes to who handles the portfolio at a meeting, I tend to take it out of any carrying case and hand it over to the art director. Since you're asking him or her to look at your work, they should decide at what pace they go through the portfolio, turning the pages themselves. If they set a leisurely pace, looking at each page carefully, try to tell them something about the piece of work they are looking at. This can be something anecdotal about the job, if the meeting is reasonably relaxed, or just a brief outline of what the piece was commissioned for, to give the work some context. Since meetings can differ radically, you need to judge whether the person viewing the portfolio is interested in your comments or not. Some prefer to make a wholly independent decision about the work and what they think about it. If the work is articulate, you don't really need to prove this verbally by explaining that it answered a particular brief.

As for your manner at a meeting, my feeling is that no one should feign liking someone if they don't. This isn't a moral standpoint; it's just that usually it's obvious when people are faking it, and that doesn't impress anyone. If you don't click with a particular person, simply stay professional and polite. Getting the tone of your interaction right is an important part of job-hunting and networking, and sometimes it needs to be worked on. If you're self-aware, you should learn through experience. Everyone is different, and you certainly can't wholly anticipate how a meeting with a complete stranger is going to go. Then there's the added pressure of wanting something from them – namely, a job. It's a matter of quiet self-confidence.

Tea packaging with illustrations by Stuart Kolakovic

Don't be tempted to puff yourself up; such bravado could well backfire and leave you seeming arrogant and self-important. Given that you've puffed yourself up to compensate for your nervousness, it would be a terrible irony to come over as quite the reverse. Be natural, friendly, not overly familiar, and not unduly fixated on getting a job out of the meeting. Look on the encounter as relationship building. It's not just about you and what you want from it.

Art buyers, directors and designers look at your work to see both whether they like it and find it interesting, and what kind of person you are. If they are in the editorial sector, they will also be looking at whether or not your work will fit their magazine. If it doesn't strike them as something they could use, remember that people move around, and that the designer in question may move on to another title within a year and be in a better position to use you. You could therefore find yourself being commissioned on the back of a meeting that took place months earlier at a completely different magazine.

It is always advisable to leave a sample, which will serve as a concise summary of what you do and how to contact you. This need not be especially elaborate or idiosyncratic. A card that can be pinned up somewhere, with a defining image from your portfolio, and your name, phone number and URL on it, is good enough. The point is to leave commissioners with something that will keep you at the front of their minds and enable them to contact you easily.

Lara Harwood's goats lorry-livery for Booths supermarkets

Having made a good impression at the meeting, don't outstay your welcome. If things are going well and you're getting on with the person you are there to see, be relaxed but don't get too settled. If they end up feeling that they have to ask you to leave because you won't stop talking, a sour note will be introduced and that's what they'll remember: the illustrator they couldn't get rid of. Afterwards, make sure you act on any promises you made. If you say you'll send additional samples to someone, ensure that you do, and not several months later. It will reinforce the good impression you've created.

Something I've also found useful is to ask if the commissioner knows anyone else who might be interested in seeing the work. My first few meetings were 'daisy-chained' by recommendations from one designer to another. Nothing opens doors like a personal recommendation. The art and design community is pretty close-knit; news of a good portfolio by an up-and-coming illustrator will soon get around. A good meeting will hopefully be fruitful beyond the duration of the meeting itself.

'Remote' job-hunting > You can also job-hunt remotely, which opens up a huge range of potential clients in many different countries. Having this range of clients based abroad can help you establish your career across several markets. Different markets have different economic circumstances, so problems you encounter in a straitened economy on your home turf can be alleviated by another country's more buoyant economy. Working for clients in different countries can be thrillingly glamorous on the surface, but it isn't risk-free. It may not necessarily present insurmountable problems, but think about all aspects of working for overseas clients and try to anticipate any difficulties in order to be better prepared to meet those challenges and reap the benefits.

The most obvious problem is the language barrier. If you are multilingual, this difficulty is reduced, but cultural differences can also impact on your dealings in a foreign marketplace. In an editorial arena, they may be less of an issue; but advertising, in its bid to reach its home market, may need someone who knows the cultural background to that market. And, even if your language skills are sufficient to accept a brief, discuss the roughs and fine-tune a finished artwork,

are they up to the task of calling an accounts department to chase the payment? Can you be sure that the rights you assume you are giving your client are the same as the ones they assume they are buying?

Reaching these other markets and the practicalities of delivering artwork have been made much easier by e-mail and the internet. You can inform clients of your existence from great distances and, assuming they are interested, they can look at your portfolio online. You can then bat e-mails back and forth and finally deliver the artwork by e-mail.

Getting hold of an individual art director's e-mail address isn't always easy, unless they want to give it to you. So, if you send them a sample in the post, provide the URL where they can check out your work and an e-mail address by which they can contact you. Once they get in touch, you then have their e-mail address, but you should treat this with respect. It is not for you to use on a daily or weekly basis, nor is it for you to pass on willy-nilly to other people. The discussion of e-mailing clients is covered in Chapter 6, but if you are in doubt, err on the side of caution when using someone's direct e-mail address.

Using the internet and e-mail for job-hunting is useful, whether your client is local or several thousand miles away, but meeting people face to face whenever possible is the best way of establishing your client base. Given how e-mail has made everyone's lives busier, this may become more difficult, but if you get the chance to make an appointment to see someone, be sure to take it. Everyone needs to pop their head above the parapet at some point, and meeting new people is refreshing for everyone and can certainly help cement business relationships.

Marc Boutavant

How did college prepare you for working as an illustrator?

> I didn't study illustration – it was considered the loser's course. You were taught to become an art director, photographer or even a visualizer, a very valuable and even honourable activity at the time! With so little idea of what to do with myself, it wasn't difficult to follow the mainstream. Fortunately, discovering great artists in Parisian libraries and sharing this with friends kept a part of my mind on illustration. It was at around this time I bought my first 'expensive' book, *Amy and Jordan* by Mark Beyer, so the idea of illustration was growing.

Can you tell me about how you began as an illustrator?

> I got work experience in an advertising agency – my portfolio was empty, but the illustrations I had at the end of this helped. I went from one work experience to another, to different agencies, and discovered the art buyers' offices were full of portfolios. It was a culture of images; the photography and illustration portfolios were inspiring. This was perhaps true of a particular generation, as most art directors came from public art schools, with 'old school' teachers. The power of the artists made a huge impression. After that, I did military service. This cut the link with agencies – when I came back to civilian life I began to work more seriously, with the help of an agent.

Are you methodical?

> I can be both methodical and messy. Children and school provide a framework, which helps. I used to waste a lot of time, but with a family to consider I get much more done in less time than I used to. Inspiration is the key, but sometimes I get a block; I don't know why, but that block works both with me and against me.

Where do you work?

> I needed a place so ended up in a studio, nicely situated on Place des Vosges. It was a bit strange, full of great people making comics at a time when comics were dead and buried for me, so I left. But after three months working at home, it was impossible to stay and talk to myself all day long. I set up a studio with friends, which drove me to continue with illustration. It was not easy at the time; I thought another life, maybe being a chef, might arrive and I would just climb into it. Now the studio makes my life more comfortable; it's better for my head and so much better for working. I also use the eyes of the others in the studio. Even if they don't look at the work, they participate in it without knowing. This enriches everything – the studio and people are part of the framework that helps me work.

What are the benefits of working from home?

> Home is efficient; you can line up jobs in an orderly queue, and manage time, but it's a bit useless for me. After a while I miss studio friends and lose my enthusiasm. I get distracted and end up fixing something around the house.

What do you like about agents?

> All they take care of, and their role as an engine, plus the feeling of not being misunderstood. They are another framework for work, and it is flattering to be represented. Sometimes, though, having an agent breaks the energizing link between me and the people who are asking me to create work. 'Break' is a bit harsh, but the 'screen' effect is not good for my motivation, though it does help, of course, when bad situations arise. I don't like to feel insulated from a client. The people who want my work are part of what drives me.

Have you had any bad experiences with clients?

> Certainly, a long time ago – not big things. A bad one I remember was a big commission, really urgent, an advertising job. I spent two days and two nights with no sleep. I was late for a meeting and they were hard and unsympathetic. I knew there was something wrong with this way of working.

How do you feel about dealing with contracts?

> I don't enjoy it, not because money is dirty, but because I don't want it to get mixed up with work. There are a lot of things to think about when working. Money issues would distance me from that.

What would be your advice to a would-be illustrator?

> It's the kind of activity you need to have a strong relationship with, to possess and be possessed by. I see it as a way of life. There's something narcissistic about this, so you need a collection of hang-ups and worries to enter what can sometimes feel like a religion.

Above: *Sport, Never Sport*, for a bag from BlueQ
Right: *Operation Pourcentage* for a French optician. The percentage price reduction was the same as the age of the child being prescribed glasses

OPÉRATION POURCENTAGE

ENFANT

VOTRE ÂGE = SON % D'ÉCONOMIE
sur sa monture

grandOptical

Right: *Look! Moon!* for *Martha Stewart Kids* magazine
Below: Flyer for 'La Guinguette Pirate'

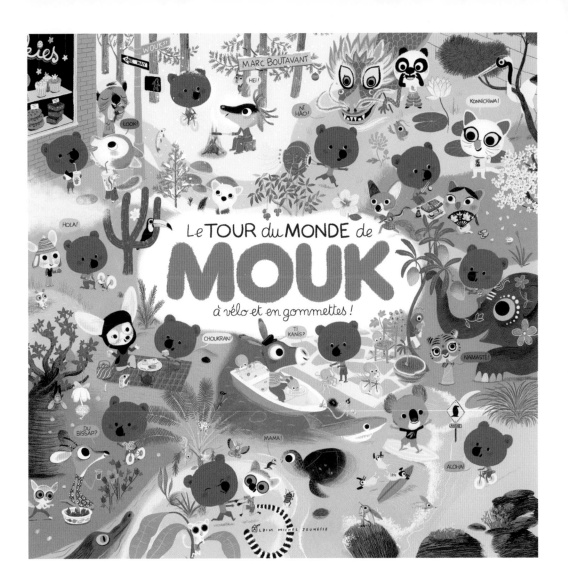

Above: *Mouk's World Tour*
Left: *Mouk in a Tuk-Tuk*

Chapter 4
Producing the first job

Getting the core information
Understanding the job
Embracing the subject
Timing and size
Fees and rights
The 'low fee' precedent
Kill fees
The learning curve
Retaining rights
Book cover commissions
Advertising commissions
Design company commissions
A final word on contracts

Getting the core information

> Let's assume, in this first instance, that despite showing your portfolio to clients from the publishing, design and advertising sectors, you've still ended up getting your first job from a magazine. Once the initial euphoria has subsided, you have the nitty-gritty realities to deal with.

People refer to getting 'the brief', which means a quantity of key information that defines what you are being asked to do, by when and for what payment. Most people consider the brief to be the copy or piece of writing that the image will illustrate, along with information about the size and shape of that image and any layout considerations, such as whether it is to run over a gutter.

First, it's likely that an art director will call to ask if you'd like to do a job for their magazine. If it's your first job, you're unlikely to be too reticent about it. Depending on who calls, you will either be given all the information you need without asking, or you will have to listen and ask questions relating to the various points you need to know about.

The core information is:

What is the story about?
When is the job needed? One deadline for roughs, one for final artwork.
What size will it be running?
How much will they pay for the illustration?

The above is the information you need to carry out the work. As a secondary consideration, you have to know whether there is a contract relating to the job and, if so, what it presumes. Given that the contract defines what exactly is being paid for, it should be considered a pivotal piece of information. But, because it's extraneous to what you need to do the work, it's easy to see it as a somewhat academic point. The contract should be considered properly, with care, as its terms should dictate whether or not you accept the job.

All the information (bar the contract) may be delivered verbally over the phone, or more usually in an e-mail, with the story or article either pasted into the body of the e-mail or as an attached document. PDFs of the layout are sometimes sent over.

In addition to the brief, you need to know what your delivery options are. E-mailing the final image is obviously the most convenient way to go. However, if it's a large file, this can cause problems. Many internal networks place firewall limitations on downloads, so you might find that your client can only accept files up to a certain size. It's best to check, so that if you need to upload a large image file to an FTP site you can get the necessary information. Alternatively, if you're in the same city, you can ask the client to send a courier to pick up a disk from you. The client may, however, expect you to courier it at your expense. If you have time you can post the file, using some form of guaranteed next-day delivery.

Returning to the practicalities of the job, you will generally need to assess quickly whether the subject matter is something you are happy to work with. I don't

A Jason Ford artwork in progress. From scribble …

mean that you have to make a moral assessment; rather, you must decide whether you can engage effectively with the subject matter and the point of view of the piece in question. (That said, we have represented people with very specific no-go areas that were distinctly moral rather than practical, and based on their religious beliefs.) In giving you a precis of the piece over the phone, a commissioner will explain what the article is about and the main point they want to convey in the illustration. The art director who is commissioning you will probably have judged that you are suitable for the piece. If you are a novice, clients are unlikely to take much of a risk on the subject matter they give you. But make up your own mind. Commissioners can get carried away when they see new, refreshing work, wanting to use you regardless of whether the subject really is a good fit for you and your work or, just as importantly, whether it's a good fit with the magazine, its look and its readership.

Understanding the job > A good example of a commissioner getting it wrong occurred a few years ago when an artist I represent did a job for a quite conservatively designed nautical magazine. In the case of this particular publication, since they were located within half a mile of our studio, I offered to take the artist's portfolio to their offices to ensure that the client understood his work, and to get a fuller sense of what was wanted from the illustration.

The subject matter seemed something that the illustrator would enjoy playing with. It was a semi-humorous piece about the practicalities of crewing yachts and the social dynamics of people cooped up with one another in a relatively small space for weeks on end, and how this often ended disastrously. I had some misgivings about the suitability of the match, but the art director, having seen the illustrator's complete portfolio, was adamant that he was right for the job.

After submission of a finished rough, the client had a very clear idea of how the piece would look, which was very much in line with the portfolio of work they had been shown. The rough was swiftly rejected by the commissioning art director and his editor on the grounds that the style did not suit the magazine's look and the readership wouldn't like it. There was no discussion about the content or idea, nor whether these fitted the piece.

When it was pointed out to them that the piece was in line with what they had been shown prior to commissioning, they simply reiterated that the style didn't suit their magazine as they usually carried cartoons, which their readership preferred. To add insult to injury they then added, 'We don't pay kill fees at this magazine.' I was flabbergasted. Given that the fee involved was reasonably small, there was no question of taking legal action, so I simply told them that we would pay the artist ourselves and that they should not call us again with a view to working with anyone we represented.

It was an extraordinary situation, arising from a client's poor understanding of illustration commissioning. Nevertheless, it provided a salutary lesson; that an art director doesn't always commission someone based on the right criteria, and that you should never take it for granted that a new client understands the matter of rejection of artwork and kill fees.

If in doubt about a commission, familiarize yourself with the magazine and think carefully about whether it fits with your work. It would probably do no harm to discuss any doubts or reservations you might have on this point with the commissioner and see what he or she thinks. I also find it's useful to ask them which piece of your work inspired them to commission you. It gives you an idea of what they have in mind before you start.

A tutor of mine once said that if he didn't grasp an idea as soon as a job was described to him, he wouldn't take it. I can relate to that sense of rapid engagement (or not) with an outline story, but sometimes a commission that looks distinctly unpromising can be a winner, once you've defined the problem and found the solution to it. So don't be put off straight away, but listen and think about it carefully and decide whether it's a subject you can work with. You don't want your first job to be the visual equivalent of the ugly sister trying to squeeze her foot into Cinderella's glass slipper. An illustrator deals with an eclectic range of subject matter, so you shouldn't necessarily decline a job simply because it doesn't quite fit with what you personally are interested in. Think of it as a more elaborate form of Pictionary. You need to be able to read an article, decide what the crux of it is and convey this in an interesting way, while hopefully bringing a little something extra to the overall spread that is more than just a visual garnish. Ideally, your image should add to, not simply repeat, what is said in the article. Together, the whole should be greater than the sum of its proverbial parts.

Embracing the subject

> The Pictionary analogy goes further, albeit in reverse (bear with me here!). As a collagist, for example, I continually collect source material and references from all sorts of places. I gather up stuff any time something catches my eye, not only when specifically hunting for a particular image for a job in hand. When I go into junk shops and charity shops, I tend to leaf through anything with pictures in it. If a book or magazine has more than a few useful images, I'll buy it. If something has one great image in it, which I reckon I can use, I'll pay well for it. Thankfully, in junk shops and so on, paying well is a relative term. The 'reverse Pictionary' analogy is the process I go through when skimming through old books and magazines. If I see a great picture, of a machine or a particular face, I think about what I could do with it and start to have ideas for uncommissioned pieces of work. Whether or not these images are ever created, it's an associative process that starts creative juices flowing and will get you

'Because the early days were so hard, I really valued getting work, and have never failed to deliver a job on time. I believe I am very lucky to earn my living this way so it's not something I take for granted.'

Michael Gillette, Illustrator

To doodle …

into the habit of gathering potentially useful material. Where you find your inspiration and references depends on the kind of illustrator you are. I know several illustrators who simply browse through a book of work by a favourite artist, just to get a colour-palette idea for an image they are working on.

I have always loved the range of subjects an illustrator may be asked to deal with in any given week – I'm a bit of a magpie in general, so reading about odd, disparate subjects appeals to me. You wouldn't necessarily choose to pick up a magazine on banking, but having been paid to read and understand an arcane piece of information about the world of banking in order to provide an illustration, you will come away from the job a little more informed (often useful when tackling crosswords). You amass quite a range of general knowledge, and you never quite know when this might come in handy. Summing up the decision-making process, you need to be up for a challenge and able to find a visual solution, but you also need to know when a subject isn't really one you want to tackle.

Timing and size > Assuming that you accept the job on the basis of the subject matter, the next crucial question is how long you have to do the job and whether you are able to do it in the time given. I think it's a challenge you have to rise to, whatever the deadline. Again, if you are a novice, it's unlikely that you would be asked to tackle something difficult in too short a time. That's a risk any art director or editor should know better than to take. However, if your work looks deceptively simple and isn't in fact as quick or easy to produce as might be imagined, be honest about that. It might be that you have to suggest a pragmatic and slightly simpler approach to meet the deadline. If you are upfront on this point, you give the commissioner the choice to proceed or cancel. Better for the client to cancel than be disappointed and reject your work because it's not as good as the piece that inspired them to offer you the job. If they choose to cancel, they will probably come back with a suitable project that has more time on it; but if you accept the commission then disappoint them, they are much less likely to call you again.

How big is the piece expected to run? This can be of negligible importance in deciding whether you can complete the job in the time allotted, but if it's a big piece, requiring lots of detail and a search for appropriate reference material, this obviously affects the amount of time you need. As you become more experienced, you may be asked to turn around work in a matter of hours. I used to think an 18-hour deadline was short, but there are plenty of jobs that have four-hour turnarounds (most commonly on newspapers).

Fees and rights > With subject matter and timing settled, you've established that you can actually do the job. The next question is the fee and what rights the publication expects.

Fees vary from publication to publication and nothing is set in stone, but there are some basic principles underpinning the fee structure. Fees are not calculated on the basis of how long it takes to create an artwork, but are usually decided on the basis of the size at which it will be reproduced in the publication, i.e. an eighth of a page (spot), a quarter, half or full page, or a double-page spread (DPS). This is because size relates to the licensing or usage of the artwork.

Generally, a piece created to run at a quarter page will be less complex than a full-page image. There are plenty of exceptions: clients sometimes want to get a lot of information or story aspects into a quarter page, or they may want a full-page piece to be very strong and simple. If there is a basic fee structure, it might be amended upwards slightly for a more complicated illustration, be it quarter or full page. Fees are not amended downwards for simpler artworks. Simplicity is the product of a lot of time spent learning how to make things simple. It is not the product of the time it takes to do a particular job.

Beyond this basic fee structure, fees can vary considerably from client to client, although there are benchmarks above or below which they can move. As I write, an average fee for a quarter-page illustration is £250 in the UK and $500 in the US. Some magazines on tighter budgets can go as low as £150 or $400 for a quarter-page illustration. Some will pay more than these average prices and this, while obviously good news, begs the question why? The answer often relates to distribution figures and where the publication is distributed. It can also involve which rights clients expect in the contract. Do they include foreign editions, or the right to sublicense the work (i.e. sell it on to a third party)?

Conversely, this doesn't necessarily apply to the lower-fee-paying magazines, many of which want extensive rights while offering very little in return. Recently, a magazine in London, which has always paid low fees, introduced a contract where none had previously existed. With no forewarning, a contract was sent to its illustrators baldly stating that fees would now cover ownership of the copyright in the artwork, as well as the artwork itself. Given that the magazine has overseas editions, which occasionally pay a nominal amount to reuse artwork, this amounted to the magazine paying less and expecting more.

This change in circumstances was not made clear when the art director commissioned two artists, both of whom had worked for the magazine before, on the understanding that it was for first, one-time rights in the UK only. The contract arrived, fortunately dated after the artwork delivery date. Initially, the art director shrugged and made half-hearted sympathetic noises, while the person responsible for rights aggressively stated that unless we signed, we wouldn't be paid. However, the contract had clearly been sent after the work had been done, and nobody can be expected to sign a contract retrospectively they don't agree with. Once the client was told that the contract wouldn't stand any kind of legal test, they backed down.

Moving forward, we at least now know what
the terms of the job are, and anyone who
agrees to work for this magazine can do
so, in the knowledge of what they will be
signing away. Most importantly, they will
have a choice in the matter.

Contract magazines, produced specifically
for internal or external distribution by
companies, sometimes pay a higher page
rate because they are more like vehicles
for corporate PR and advertising than fully
fledged consumer magazines. Again, fees
will depend on who the client is and for
whom the magazine is being produced.
I say that they only sometimes pay more,
as there is a growing trend for design

companies and publishers involved in producing contract magazines to call
these publications 'magazines' in order to have them considered as consumer
magazines and be able to pay lower fees accordingly.

You can negotiate on the fee with both consumer and contract magazines.
Each situation is different. You may get an art director who is happy to offer the
maximum he or she can, in which case it's likely to be a 'take it or leave it' offer.
Alternatively, you may get one who always begins by offering as low a fee as
possible, either to allow for more budget elsewhere or simply to win brownie
points by bringing the magazine in under budget. If the latter is the case, there
may be some latitude to push the fee upwards, even if only marginally. One
unique aspect of each situation is the interpersonal chemistry and how you ask
for more money. I've found that most art directors are happy enough to have the
conversation – although none appreciates whining about fees – but some treat
their budget as if it were their own money and resent any kind of request for a
higher fee. (In some cases, it is literally their own money; if it's a design company
that has an overall budget for a contract magazine, anything saved on illustration
or other fees goes straight to its bottom line – i.e. its profitability.) In an ideal
world, any fee negotiations should be conducted with a view to achieving a win–
win situation for all concerned. If you don't feel underpaid and the client doesn't
feel overcharged, everyone is happy, making for good customer relations and,
ultimately, good business.

If you are a relative newcomer to illustration, some clients will try to offer you
less, simply because they'll assume you don't know the rates. They'll tell you that
it's all they have in the budget and that, while the fee is low for the quantity of
work, it's 'an opportunity to raise your profile'. This argument can be used
by anyone, on anyone, regardless of their experience. It's usually a weak one,
used as a wilting fig leaf for the poorly endowed budget. However, for the
relative newcomer such an argument, while a poor excuse for a low fee, should
be factored into the consideration of whether to take the job or not.

The 'low fee' precedent　> Something that always troubles me about a low-fee job is the precedent it sets. Sometimes, even if you know the money is poor, you also know it could take you as little as three hours to do the illustration; therefore, as an hourly wage, it works out quite well. However, as touched on above, fees are not calculated on a 'work for hire' hourly rate basis, but on the basis of licensed usage of your artwork. In that respect, doing work for lower than respectable fees can set dangerous precedents that have much wider ramifications.

First, it suggests to publishers that people are willing to work for those less-than-respectable fees, so why should they increase them? Ask any illustrator about how much they are paid and, unfortunately, most will launch into a tirade about the fact that fees have not increased in 10 or 15 years. Sadly it's true. While everything else has risen in price, illustration fees haven't, so in real terms they've gone down and down. If people don't occasionally say no to the fees offered, the publisher in question never has any reason to consider raising them. But if art directors are finding it difficult to get people to work for the payments they can offer, they will have to tell the publisher that they are having problems, and a bit more money will be made available.

Secondly, if one magazine is getting away with paying low fees, why should another publication offer to pay more? The result is a downward pressure on fees, which may, at best, not go any lower, but certainly won't rise. I'm sure that some people are uncomfortable with worrying about how much they'll be paid and want to concern themselves with the 'art'. Unfortunately, the two are intrinsically linked. If fees are eroded, so is your ability to make a living as a professional illustrator.

Illustrators often discuss fees, even if only in general terms. Those who know one another well are more likely to talk about specifics, particularly if obvious disparities arise. If you get a chance, discuss the fees you are offered with someone more experienced than yourself and you'll find out soon enough whether you're getting paid roughly the right amount, a bit less, a lot less or maybe even a bit more than some others (it does happen). Alternatively, you can always contact your national illustration society for advice. It should be able to give you an idea of the kinds of rates being paid for different kinds of work. It will probably provide a reasonable benchmark for editorial and possibly publishing rates, but may be less reliable on design and advertising, where rates and budgets vary a good deal more. Ultimately, it's a commercial negotiation to see if you can work within a proposed budget, but there should still be a rough benchmark, to let you know whether you are operating on par or under par with industry norms.

Kill fees　> Kill fees, offered when work is rejected, are a difficult subject to give firm advice on. Terms of business usually refer to kill fees amounting to 50 per cent of the full payment when work is turned down on or after delivery of rough artwork, and 100 per cent if rejection happens on delivery of final artwork. This is a generally accepted approach that seems to be an industry standard. The assumption here is that, having had specific feedback at rough stage, this advice

To a bit of character development …

has been actioned and the work completed; therefore a full fee is payable. Reality is more nuanced and often requires some dexterity and subtle negotiation to resolve. While an illustrator's or agent's terms might state such percentages, in reality you may well have to work with circumstances dictated by individual situations. Such terms ultimately reflect the best of outcomes and, to be fair, in my experience the majority of clients do seem to operate on the basis of similar terms. It's the one or two that don't that will test your mettle and negotiating skills. If a fee is big enough, you may find it worthwhile going to court to enforce your terms, rather than allow yourself to be bullied into accepting derisory kill fees.

The learning curve > Just as each piece that gets into print is a good advertisement for you, work also provides learning opportunities. I don't know any illustrator who is totally happy with any job he or she does. There's always an element of self-critique: 'I should have left that out or made it smaller', or 'If it hadn't been quite such a rush, I would have liked to have done this or that.' Ultimately, the deadline bell rings and it's game over. The art director may well be pleased, but you might feel differently. This is normal and is generally quite a healthy outlook. Not long after I began working, I did a lot of illustrations for computer magazines. Very often they were needed for repetitive features on new software or operating systems, and I started to get frustrated until I realized that this provided a good proving ground for trying out different things in my work. If a feature was almost identical to one I'd illustrated two weeks earlier, it was a chance to try again and offer a different – or, ideally, improved – solution. It not only paid the bills but also gave me a great chance to develop the work without worrying too much about it.

Each job you do, on time, with a satisfied client at the end, is a confidence booster. Although this might sound a bit inane, I think everyone needs this sort of boost now and again; and if you're a novice, just starting to get a career off the ground, you need such boosts to carry you through potentially difficult times.

Retaining rights > A relatively unobtrusive way in which an illustrator's ability to sustain a career can be eroded is via the rights question. The rights some clients try to include within a fee go way beyond those that they require for the specific job that has been commissioned.

Generally, you should operate on the basis that you're providing an illustration for the job you've been commissioned to do. If someone asks you for a quarter-page artwork for a particular magazine, which is published in a certain country, then that's what it should say in the contract. This is normally expressed as 'First, one-time use in [territory name, i.e. UK, US, France etc.] only'. This means the magazine gets to be the first publication to print the piece of work (i.e. the work has not appeared anywhere else beforehand), and to use it once only and in the specific territory where it's published. As you retain copyright, you extend to the magazine an exclusivity period of usually 90 days from the date of first publication, after which time you are entitled, if you so wish or have the opportunity, to license this work to another publication for a reuse fee.

In reality, many contracts stipulate reproduction rights that are far more extensive. They often push to have first rights, exclusive for 90 days, and thereafter non-exclusive rights to use the image in other editions of the magazine and/or to be able to sell the rights to use your image to third parties. Many magazines offer small fees for running your image in the same editorial context in an overseas edition. Less reputable ones are now trying to have that right thrown in, so you begin to lose money from the outset. If they have the right to sell your work on to third parties, the more ethical magazines will include details of a fee split for these sales. Since they are the ones who find the buyer, so to speak, I have less of a problem with this, although I generally prefer to score through these details in the contract. Again, less reputable magazines will say they retain the right to sell work on, but nowhere mention any payment to you. By selling work on, they may well end up making more money from your image than they paid to you in fees.

Sometimes these magazines state that you retain the copyright in the artwork, but that they have exclusive rights to publish it, so in practical terms it's nothing more than nominal ownership for you. Alternatively, dispensing with any pretence, they may insist that the copyright in the work is theirs, and that you have no rights to it, once you have handed it in.

Someone once asked me whether there was a 'goodwill' factor in giving a client copyright. While I can understand that magazines may be facing tough competition in the fight for circulation and are, of necessity, looking for ways to increase their revenue, I can't think of any instance when a smaller business should give a larger business a valuable asset for nothing.

The whole issue of contracts and precedents can be traced back to Condé Nast Publications, which, notoriously, retained ownership of artwork and copyright in their contracts. Many magazines decided to follow that particular business model and demanded similar rights. Condé Nast have largely softened their position and will negotiate on certain points, but they started a trend that does not work in the illustrator's (or photographer's) favour. Ownership of copyright was hard won when first fought for by Magnum Photographers in the 1950s, but it can be quietly eroded unless it is heeded and defended by everyone.

On a more positive note, contracts need not be set in stone; and while many can appear draconian, if you are prepared to question or discuss certain points, it is possible to win concessions on many of the worst ones. This is covered in Chapter 5, but it's important to know that you may be required to sign a

Some refining of the composition …

contract when you agree to do a job. It may come after the event, with the rather dubious practice of insisting that you sign a contract you have never seen before, or else you will not be paid. It's therefore best to ask early whether there is a contract and, if so, whether you can see it straight away or have it sent to you with the brief via e-mail. Never bury your head in the sand. These matters don't go away, but get more complicated. If you know the deal upfront, you have the choice of doing the job, arguing the contract and gaining concessions on some unsatisfactory points, or simply declining the job on the basis of the contract. This final option is a tough call when starting out, but if people continually roll over and concede to unfair

contracts, everyone's rights are eroded and, in time, illustration as a professional activity will not be viable. It will be relegated to something a few desperate graduates do until they can find a more lucrative option, and another set of desperate graduates replaces them. There is a bigger picture, which you need to understand if you are to be a serious and dedicated professional illustrator.

Alternatives to editorial work as 'first jobs' come from publishing, advertising and design, probably in that order of probability in Europe; in the US, I'd shift advertising to the least likely of possibilities.

Book cover commissions

> Book publishing illustrations used to work roughly to a one-month turnaround. You might be given the book (if it was being 'repackaged' or reissued), or a manuscript to read, with the expectation of receiving ideas, sketches and so on about two weeks after that. You would get feedback on those and be given a further two weeks to produce final artwork. This still happens occasionally, but you are just as likely to get a synopsis to work with via the book's editor. Alternatively, the jacket designer or publisher may prefer to give you a precise description of what they want and expect you to go away and artwork that. This is the 'glove puppet' school of commissioning, and isn't very satisfying.

Some publishers have started to commission covers with the proviso that you show them artwork when it is 75 to 90 per cent finished. They can see what they are going to get, but retain the right to kill the job at that point for 50 per cent of the fee. In other words, you are expected to do nearly all the work, but they can still change their minds about choosing you and your work. I think this reflects the growing power of the sales and marketing department, which can reject covers – this necessitates a rethink for the art department, which tackles the problem by getting as finished a piece as possible to pitch to sales. The extra work is shouldered by the illustrator for a fee that flies in the face of normal practice.

When asked to work in this way, you can either produce a 'rough' for the cover meeting, for the 50 per cent fee (although there will still be an intermediate stage for discussion), or you can try to negotiate the fee percentage according to the level of finish that is required before a decision is made on the choice of cover art. Such an approach isn't set in stone, so your negotiating powers may not be honed sufficiently to get the commissioner to be this flexible.

Advertising commissions

> How frequently illustration is used in advertising varies a great deal from country to country. European agencies are currently using a lot of illustration across various types of campaign, while in the US I would say that, in general, it is used less often. Given the size of the US market, in relative terms the UK in particular uses a huge amount. If you do get asked to work for an advertising agency, it is likely to be to quite a prescriptive brief that has been approved by various people along the way. You are generally given a visual as a brief, which takes the form of a quick marker-pen sketch of the idea or something more elaborately rendered. Your job is to go away and execute this in your own way, in line with your portfolio. You may be briefed in person by an art director or the art buyer, or you may get everything sent via e-mail and be briefed over the phone. Unlike for an editorial job, purchase orders are everything. You should try to get one before starting work. While this isn't always practical (often because of prevailing internal bureaucracy), try to get whatever fee and terms of use you agree to in writing, if not on a purchase order, then in an e-mail.

While the brief is prescriptive, the fees are a great deal higher than for most other kinds of work. For instance, in the UK you can expect between £4000 and £5000 for a one-year national press advertisement that runs in the UK only. However, depending on the client, the importance of the campaign and so on, the fee can fall as low as, say, £3000. Usually, you should try to break it down into artworking and licensing fees, split very roughly 50/50. That way, if the ad doesn't run for any reason, you still know what you're getting for artworking. It's very difficult to go into a great deal of detail on advertising fees because they are so complicated. There are also many different scenarios and mitigating circumstances that can dictate higher or lower ones.

When dealing with advertising agencies, there's generally a huge sense of urgency. There may be plenty of deliberating in the run-up to kick-off, but when things do get underway, the work is usually wanted immediately. Two weeks of deliberation, followed by two days in which to get the artwork finished, is typical. You will usually be expected to show some kind of interim stage, as in any other kind of job, before supplying the final artwork. Thereafter, tweaking may be needed before it's accepted.

Bearing in mind how many people are often involved in making decisions in an advertising campaign, after initial contact, checking on your availability and so on, you could be kept waiting for days or even weeks before a job actually starts. Alternatively, there may be no news – complete silence – until you find out that the agency has dropped the idea and gone with something entirely different,

To the final drawing, to which he will then add colour

neglecting to tell you. For this reason, I never count on any advertising job until it's done and billed for. It's the nature of the beast.

Design company commissions

> While you can be commissioned for logo design or packaging work, the most common job to come from a design company is probably illustration for a client's brochure or annual report. Both documents will generally need to convey something about the organization's corporate culture, and it may well be decided to illustrate this.

In many respects, this kind of job resembles an editorial one, in that you need to read, digest and distill a piece of text and come up with a visual accompaniment. The difference is likely to be in the approval and fine-tuning process. While an editorial illustration accompanies a feature or short article in a magazine, its significance and lifespan are relatively short, in that it is likely to be a fairly light piece that is forgotten once the next issue comes out. An image in a corporate brochure needs to keep working, reinforcing what the company wants to say about itself. While not exactly branding, it is closely related to how the company perceives itself, hence the need, often, to fine-tune the image, to ensure it says what it is supposed to say about the company. Another difference – a positive one – is that because of its importance to the end-user, greater care is taken over the design and layout, so your illustration should appear in a more sensitively designed context. As with everything, there are exceptions: I've seen beautifully designed editorial pages and dreadful-looking corporate brochures.

Fees for this kind of work vary, but depending on the size at which the image is to run, its complexity and the print run of the document, you might receive anything from £1000 to £3000 for an inside illustration ($3000 to $8000 per image in the US). Again, there are many variables involved and each client has a different budget, so much comes down to discussion and negotiation.

A final word on contracts

> All jobs will have contractual issues to consider. While publishing work may have contracts similar to editorial work, advertising and design more often entail setting down what you are agreeing to before starting work. Much can be done by confirming in an e-mail your understanding of what you are being asked to do, for what fee, and how the client intends to use the image you produce, including any limitations on that use. If it's an advertising job, for one year's national press use in the UK only, this needs to be said in your confirming e-mail. It's always worth reiterating that the copyright remains yours, and that any additional usage would need to be negotiated and agreed. You can't then be accused of not being clear about your understanding of the job you're agreeing to.

Michael Gillette

How did college prepare you for working as an illustrator?

> I was absolutely unprepared, embarrassingly so. Partly because I never really saw myself as an illustrator. I didn't like what illustration had become in the 1980s and couldn't see how I was going to fit in with the prevailing mood. It was also, truth be told, because there wasn't a whole lot of discussion about what was going to happen in the outside world.

Can you tell me about your experiences on leaving?

> The only thing I felt I had a depth of knowledge in was music, so my first jobs related to that. In college I felt I was a graphic designer, so on leaving I started doing sleeves, creating design and image together; this was my USP. Regular illustration work I had zero luck with. I was making everything up as I went along, changing tack regularly. I decided I was going to do serious work, then realized that humour was important to me and I should incorporate it into my work. I was like a headless chicken. It was also the height of the recession so it was a bleak time.

Are you methodical?

> Yes, I am. Because the early days were so hard, I really valued getting work, and have never failed to deliver a job on time. I believe I am very lucky to earn my living this way so it's not something I take for granted.

What are the benefits of working from home?

> Mostly financial. Moving to San Francisco, I rented somewhere big enough to live and work in, in the area I wanted. I probably couldn't have done that with the added cost of a studio. Also, I often work long hours, so my wife would never see me if I had a studio. But I did learn in a studio that we all face the same challenges. I saw others getting bothered about what, in the scheme of things, were minor irritations; it allowed me to detect that quality in myself and try to curb those habits. And I learned computer know-how and business skills from those around me.

Do you have an agent?

> Yes, I do. I like having someone I can trust who is on my side. When jobs get to a certain size I think you need that help. Dislikes: there is always the percentage! I've had three different agents, two didn't work out that well; in those cases you're better off on your own.

Do you let your agent take care of promotion?

> In the first years of my career I learnt to promote myself. My first agent got me very little work, so I carried on regardless, and never stopped. Because agents have so many other artists, they are never going to be able to tell your full story. If you leave everything to them, you may not get very far. That's my experience; maybe other illustrators are easier to sell.

What role does your website fulfil for you?

> I've had it for seven years, and it's had a profound influence on my career. I get thousands of visitors a month, and not all of them are my mum. I've always tried to do varied work, and I need breadth to show it in a sympathetic way. My website has solved that. It's allowed me to show work I wouldn't previously have been able to promote, and so has allowed me to grow. A lot of clients come directly to me because they have heard about my website; for the most part I refer them back to my agent.

Do you turn work down?

> If I think it will make me feel a lesser artist, the pay is too poor or I get a feeling in my gut, I avoid.

What do you like most about being an illustrator? What do you like least?

> They are really the same things, viewed from different angles. You have no boss, which is great, but you have to motivate yourself constantly. You can't coast, which seems to be a big part of having a real job. Illustration is mainly a solitary occupation, and that can be hard. I read that, as a creative career, it's like digging a tunnel with a fork. It can be joyous to live without the irritation of people's mind games, agendas and general bad behaviour. I think the root of it is that you are in control of your life – terrifying at times, extremely liberating at others. I almost never turn off thinking about work. Thankfully I like my work. To live life doing something you have little interest in would be destructive.

What would be your one piece of advice?

> Set goals, and ask every day 'What have I done to achieve these things?' Rinse and repeat.

Above left: *Being Bond* cover
Above right: Cover for a German translation of Ian Fleming's *Thunderball*
Right: Identity for Zoo Films

Opposite, above: For *Dwell* magazine
Opposite, below left: *Anonymous was a Woman* for *Yale* magazine
Opposite, below right: *Herman Cain* for the *New York Times*
Right: *Ego* (personal work)
Below: Backdrop for Rumer tour

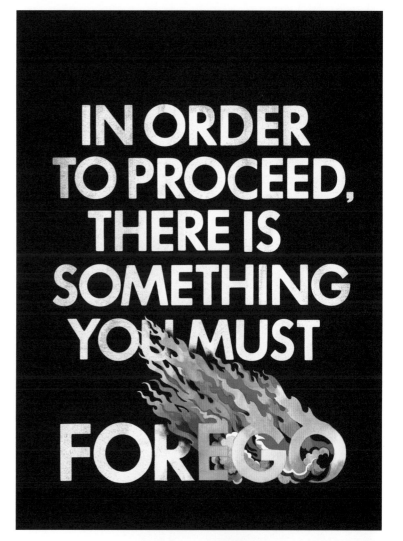

Chapter 5
Billing it – financial tips

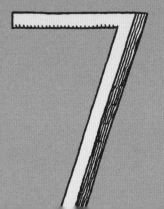

Invoices

> When I handed in my first commissioned piece of work, the art director asked if I had brought along an invoice. I confessed to having no idea what an invoice was or what I needed to say on it. She very kindly took a piece of blank paper and showed me where to write my address, where to put the magazine's address, what I had to say on it, where I put the amount and where I numbered the invoice. She then duly photocopied it and gave me the copy, retaining the original, which she sent to the accounts department. I can't recall now whether I needed to chase that payment or if it came through within a month or so.

Once your first job is done, you too will need to submit a bill or invoice to the client, so that they can pay you. It needs to have any mandatory client reference numbers on it, so that it can be passed along a chain of people within that company for authorization, which should culminate in a fairly prompt payment in the form of a cheque or by direct transfer into your bank account.

Given the quantity of invoices I handle these days, both those generated and sent out by the agency and those sent to us by artists and suppliers, I've seen all types and formats of invoice, but they all need to have the same basic information on them as standard, plus any additional references that correspond to various accounting systems.

The essential information needed on any invoice is pretty straightforward. It can be said to consist of six basic questions. Who is it from? When is it dated? Who is it to? What is it for? How much is it for? What are the payment terms?

Only occasionally will invoices from my agency's represented illustrators come in to us with the kind of detail that we as an agency use when invoicing clients on the artist's behalf. Such detail is more important when an artist is VAT registered (VAT being a sales tax applied in Europe). In most cases, provided we know the 'What is it for?' part (to which of our clients the illustrator's invoice refers to), the illustrator doesn't need to detail exactly what was supplied and with what reproduction rights, as this is already covered on our invoice to the client. However, when you are supplying an invoice directly to a client, you really need to include as much information on it as possible. It's good practice to establish good habits from the outset, so take your business and accounts seriously. I've suggested below the kind of 'answers' you should give to the six basic invoice 'questions'.

Who is it from?

> This is straightforward enough: state your name and full address. It is best if the name is that of the person to whom the cheque is payable and the address is where the payment should be sent. Some people use a pseudonym or trading name for their work, but still need to be paid in their real name. If there is a difference, you can stipulate who the cheque is made payable to at the bottom of the invoice, where payment terms are stated.

When is it dated?

> Somewhere on your invoice, you need to put its date, sometimes referred to as 'tax point'. This, unless otherwise agreed, is the date that your artwork was delivered and accepted as final, finished artwork that fulfilled the brief. This is also the date by which you 'age' your invoice. Whatever payment terms are in place, they refer to the number of days after this date. From a tax perspective, the tax point or date is when you did the work and when it should be factored into your accounts, either for income tax purposes or for VAT purposes if you are VAT registered.

Tracking your invoices

> Somewhere near the date, you should have an invoice number. This is your reference number, and all invoices, for any work you do, should be numbered sequentially in chronological order. Needless to say, you must keep copies of all invoices issued, and keeping all your financial records in good order will save a lot of headaches later on.

Start by creating a common-sense system that you can follow from the outset, which allows you to track any financial paperwork in a logical way. Ultimately, you may rely on an accountant to deal with your system, so it's good to get it into shape straight away. My own system consisted of a red accounts book, arranged chronologically in months, with a column on the left for the date and the next column for the invoice number, followed by a column for the client name, then the three fee columns left to right: gross, sales tax or VAT, and net. Even if you're not yet VAT registered, it's good to build a column in, just in case. The last column was 'date paid'. By recording invoices in date order, running down the page, I could add the next sequential invoice number and keep the chronology and sequential number in step. This may sound obvious, but I have received bundles of invoices from illustrators that have later dates coupled with earlier invoice numbers, which is not good practice.

'I think bad experiences revolve around some sort of communication failure. I've been lucky to work for the most part with really great, understanding people.'

Sam Weber, Illustrator

In my accounts book I could see at a glance how many jobs I had done and how much I had billed each month. Also, by comparing invoice dates with the 'date paid' column, I could see how long it was taking to get paid. If you start working for a client on a regular basis, you can quickly see roughly how long it takes for them to pay you. This is important for some semblance of cash-flow management.

For the copies of my invoices, I had two folders; one marked 'Invoices Unpaid' and one marked 'Invoices Paid'. As each payment came in, the corresponding invoice was shifted over to the Invoices Paid folder. Additional information that's useful to keep with your copy of an invoice is a copy of any contract or purchase order pertaining to the job. This way, if you need to refer to that information, you can easily trace it by invoice number. When the payment comes through, by cheque or bank transfer, it should be accompanied by a remittance advice, with details of

the payment being made to you by that particular client. Attach this to your invoice and mark the date it was received, before filing it in Invoices Paid.

A simple system like this can be adapted to deal with VAT should you ever need to register for it. If you create a similar system for dealing with bills sent to you, you'll stay on top of everything more easily. It will also help your accountant, and the less time he or she spends trying to figure out messily kept records, the less you'll pay in accountant's fees.

Getting back to the matter of creating an invoice for a client, the next item is …

Who is it to?

> Your invoice should be addressed to your client contact name, be it the art director or editor, with their address. Occasionally, you may be asked to post it directly to an accounts payable address, so once a job is finished ask who the invoice should be sent to and check that it's the address you delivered the artwork to. If in doubt about anything, always ask.

What is it for?

> This needs to cover what you supplied to the person you are billing. Was it a colour or black-and-white artwork? If it's an editorial commission, you need to state the size at which the artwork is supposed to run in the publication. This is a salient point because pricing is partly dependent on it. You could arguably produce a piece of work that could run over a quarter page or a full page, but the difference would be the size at which it ran when printed. The fee could be £250 (or US $500) for a quarter-page image, or £400 plus (or US $1500 plus) if it were to run as a full page, and this would not be affected by how long it took you to do the piece or how complicated it was. In this instance, it's about usage.

If you have supplied several artworks for one feature, you may be asked to provide a breakdown of the fees, e.g. one full-colour full-page artwork at one price and three full-colour quarter-page artworks at another, each with the sum of those fees and then their total as the amount you are invoicing for.

You should also detail the story, article or feature that an illustration was prepared for, with its working title. If possible, give the issue of the publication it is expected to run in. After this, it's useful to state the kind of licence you are granting. Is it for 'first, one-time use, UK [or whichever territory the publication is being distributed in] only, 90 days exclusive'? This will be explained later in the chapter, as it is not straightforward, in much the same way that so-called payment terms aren't.

Client references

> Under this section of your invoice, there may be a job reference or purchase order number that needs to be quoted. It used to be that only design or advertising companies used purchase orders, but many editorial clients now use this system. Again, when you are ready to bill, check whether a purchase order or any internal reference number is needed.

Job numbers These are usually a client's internal billing reference. If a company is incurring costs or buying goods and services in the process of working for its own client, it attaches a job number to all the orders for work that it issues, so it can track the expenditure and pass those costs on to its client. These numbers are more often used by design and advertising companies, and usually in conjunction with a purchase order number.

Purchase order numbers Much as you will order and number your invoices sequentially, purchase orders are there for clients to track their expenditure. Most are tied to internal computer systems that require the art director, designer or art buyer to set you up as a vendor (or seller of services). Their expenditure on you will then be authorized in the form of a purchase order number. Since purchase orders are part of a payment

authorization process, if a company uses them and you don't have one, it will make getting paid more complicated. You should also read any physical purchase orders you receive, as terms of business are often stated on them. Make sure you check these terms and that you agree with them, otherwise you could find yourself inadvertently agreeing to less than favourable ones that assume rights you were not intending to relinquish.

Commissioner's authorized number A few publications now operate on either a purchase order number (PO#) or a PO# coupled with a number identifying the commissioner, who has the authority to agree fees and buy your services. Again, it's an internal client accounting reference, but if their system uses it, make sure the right numbers appear on your invoices if you want to get paid in a timely fashion.

It's a good idea to state the purchase order number either near your invoice number or right next to the 'invoice' heading, where it can't be missed. If you fail to put on the invoice any client reference number that the accounts payable department uses, payment will not happen. The accounts department may well not call to tell you that it is missing; they simply won't process the invoice.

You might find this out only when you call up to ask when you're getting paid, which might be a month or so after you finished the job and invoiced for it. You then find out that your invoice is 'not on the system' because there's no authorization for it since it's missing the purchase order number. You must then go back to the person who commissioned you and hope they can provide the purchase order number, and you may be asked to resubmit your invoice with that number on it. You can in some instances expect to start the waiting process all over again. So, by failing to include all the information needed for the client's accounting system, you will have doubled your wait for payment. This might mean that what should normally be a six-week waiting time is extended to 12 weeks. That's 12 weeks of bills coming in and not being able to pay them. That may involve explanatory phone calls to

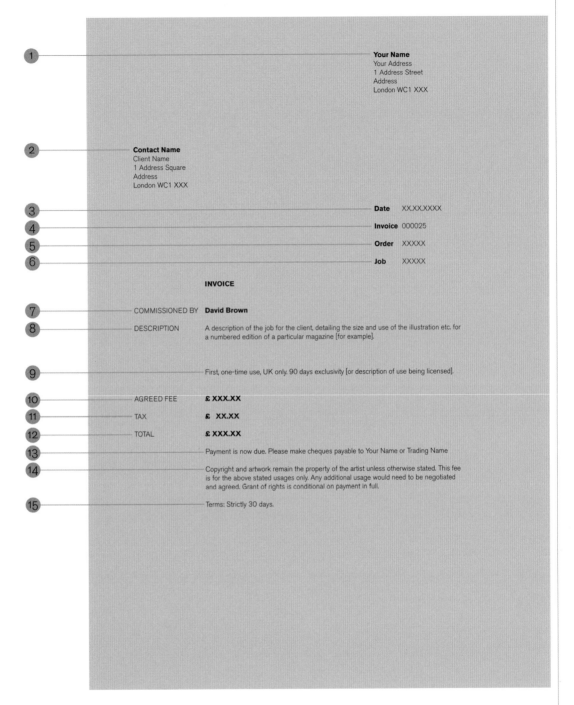

Your Name
Your Address
1 Address Street
Address
London WC1 XXX

Contact Name
Client Name
1 Address Square
Address
London WC1 XXX

Date XX.XX.XXXX

Invoice 000025

Order XXXXX

Job XXXXX

INVOICE

COMMISSIONED BY **David Brown**

DESCRIPTION   A description of the job for the client, detailing the size and use of the illustration etc. for a numbered edition of a particular magazine [for example].

First, one-time use, UK only. 90 days exclusivity [or description of use being licensed].

AGREED FEE   **£ XXX.XX**

TAX   **£ XX.XX**

TOTAL   **£ XXX.XX**

Payment is now due. Please make cheques payable to Your Name or Trading Name

Copyright and artwork remain the property of the artist unless otherwise stated. This fee is for the above stated usages only. Any additional usage would need to be negotiated and agreed. Grant of rights is conditional on payment in full.

Terms: Strictly 30 days.

A sample invoice
1 > Your name and address 2 > Client's name and address 3 > Date 4 > Invoice no.
5 > Purchase order no. 6 > Job no. 7 > Commissioner 8 > Description 9 > Rights
10 > Fee 11 > VAT/sales tax 12 > Total 13 > Payment instructions 14 > Grant of licence
15 > Payment terms

fend off your creditors, which is all stress that in many instances can be avoided.

How much is it for?

> The fee is stated after the client references section. It should be given as a total of the fees due, even if you have already provided a breakdown of fees in your description of what the invoice is for. If you are not VAT registered, this is simply a one-line total entitled 'total due'. If you are VAT registered, it's a three-line job. The first line gives the 'agreed fee', which is the total amount due to you, not including any VAT. The second line states VAT as a percentage due on top of the fees. Your third and final line is the 'total', which is the sum of your agreed fees plus VAT.

All discussions about fees will be exclusive of VAT. Nobody ever tries to discuss them from a perspective where VAT is included. It is always an additional amount that is due on top of agreed fees, and is chargeable by you if you become VAT registered.

With regard to VAT, you can register for it voluntarily, in which case you are responsible for charging VAT on your invoices at the appropriate rate and then paying that money to HM Revenue & Customs on a monthly or quarterly basis. In turn, you can claim back business-related VAT you have paid out in the same period. If your business turnover exceeds a certain level, VAT registration becomes mandatory in many countries, including the UK and mainland Europe, and you can then be fined for failing to register in a timely fashion.

If you are unsure about any aspect of your financial responsibilities, check the rules that apply to you, either by visiting your national tax authority's website, or by seeking advice from an accountant, to see precisely what is required.

Payment terms

> Below the fee section you can include two statements. The first concerns your stated ownership of the artwork and copyright. The second gives your payment terms, i.e. the length of time you are giving the client to pay your invoice. It's useful to state that the grant of any usage rights that you are licensing to the client is made on the condition of your invoice being paid in full. It rarely affects when clients pay you, but if an invoice becomes seriously overdue you can draw their attention to this statement. It will make them aware that if they have published your work without paying you, they are technically in breach of your copyright, and you could then take legal action against them on that basis. The reality is rarely quite so straightforward, but it can help

An early Tom Gauld invoice

focus an accounts department's attention on your unpaid bill.

Unfortunately, when you get paid rarely has anything to do with your stated terms. With editorial clients, the payment cycle is usually tied to the issue date of the edition of the magazine your illustration will appear in. An average wait for payment from a magazine is about six weeks, depending on what date during the month you invoice. If whoever is responsible for passing invoices to the accounts department is at all tardy or disorganized, your invoice can go astray or get separated from the others pertaining to the issue of the magazine that the accounts department is paying. If this happens, you may not know about it until you call to check on how your invoice is doing.

Design companies are most likely to pay you once they have been paid by their client. On average, expect a wait of two months. Advertising agencies, sometimes because they are awaiting payment from their client, generally take about the same length of time. It is not unusual for either of them to hit the three-month mark before they pay your invoice. Invoices can go five or six months before they are paid.

Checking with accounts departments is always advisable – that way you should at least know whether your invoice is on the system and is in line to be paid. If it isn't on the system or there's a problem, it's better to start dealing with this sooner rather than later.

One thing you can sometimes do in negotiating fees for a design or advertising job is agree a slightly lower fee on the proviso that it's paid within 14 or 30 days from invoice. If you get this agreement, make sure that it's stated on any purchase order, so you can draw a disbelieving accounts department's attention to the fact. We as an agency have done this on various occasions, with a 70 per cent rate of honour and a 30 per cent rate for not sticking to the agreement. I've learned that one way of getting an accounts department to focus on the agreement is to bill for the higher amount and state that a discount is granted if payment is made within 14 or

30 days, whatever was agreed. Otherwise, it's easy enough for the accounts department to ignore the agreed terms, pay you the lower amount and take 60 days to pay it. If that happens, what can you really do?

Following up and chasing payment

> Once you've submitted your invoice, you can take a passive position (if you can afford to financially) and wait for payment to turn up. But it pays to get into the habit of calling accounts departments, even if it's just to check that your invoice is on their system and that they know you are owed money. Thereafter, you can ask them when you can expect the payment. In calling accounts departments, you can ask whether they prefer to pay by cheque or bank transfer. While having that conversation, you can ask how long it normally takes for an invoice to be processed and paid, and whether it matters on what date in the month you bill.

Some accounts departments pay according to their own cycles – for example, the end of the month after the one in which the invoice was submitted. In that instance, if you bill on the twenty-eighth of the month, you'll probably be paid around that date the following month. If, however, you bill on, say, the fifth of the month, you will still have to wait until the twenty-eighth of the following month, so the delay in being paid is extended by three weeks. Other accounts departments will pay on publication, and pay all invoices relating to a particular issue at the same time. If you delay billing or the art director doesn't pass your invoice on to accounts in good time, it can fall through the net. Then it's a matter of hassling the accounts department to pay it in the next cheque run. Unless it's a publication in difficulty, editorial clients tend to pay on a regular basis, since their product is regular. There are plenty of exceptions to these rules: one London-based publisher of business titles pays only after 90 days (three months!) and is not embarrassed about it.

I have always found it useful to get to know, if not the faces, then the names and voices of the people in various accounts departments. When you submit your invoice, ask the commissioner who you should contact if you need to chase up payment.

When you call up a particular accounts department on a regular basis, ask for people by name, so you can start developing a cordial working relationship with them. Wherever possible, avoid taking out any frustrations you might have about delays in payment on the individuals in the accounts department. They are key to sending that payment out to you, and you need to do as much as possible to get them on your side. Getting angry with them and demanding a payment is likely to ensure that your invoice goes to the bottom of the pile or gets lost.

The opposite approach is to remain calm and explain that you are a freelancer and that you are waiting for a payment that you really need. Can they tell you what is happening with your invoice? If they tell you, for example, that so-and-so needs to authorize the payment, ask if there is anything they can do to help get it authorized as soon as possible. If you can strike up a good rapport with an accounts person, the chances are they'll do their best to help you. In some cases you will need the patience of a saint, because one or two individuals will take a perverse pleasure in saying no, just to annoy you. Sad, but they do exist. All I can say is try the charm offensive and lose your temper at your peril.

'Unless it is a very complicated contract, I can deal with it on my own. English is not even my first language, so contracts are not too bad.'

Yuko Shimizu,
Illustrator

In both instances, if you feel payment is being delayed or is particularly late, you can mention the fact that if your work has been used already, technically the company is in breach of copyright. This should always be done calmly but emphatically, with the inference that you might have to look at other means of getting paid. Involving solicitors is generally not worthwhile for smaller sums of money, and I would say you should never threaten anyone with this. If you are going to seek legal advice, say so, but again, don't say you are going to 'take legal action' unless you really are going to do so. Never threaten something and then not follow through.

If you are considering legal action, get advice and then weigh up whether it's worth it. To be honest, it rarely comes to that; it's mostly a matter of cajoling money out of slow payers, rather than taking them to court.

There is a common misconception – if you can call it that – in some accounts departments that they can respond to your claim that your payment is overdue by saying their payment terms are 60 or 90 days, or whatever they deem them to be. When this happened to me, I calmly pointed out that as I was extending them credit, I ought to decide payment terms – just as a credit card company does. When a credit card company lends you money, you can't tell them you'll only pay the bill every 60 or 90 days. This suggestion didn't get me anywhere. I think the accounts department in question was really talking about its payment cycles, but it was a little nonplussed at my retort.

However, when you bill a client you are effectively lending them money, by providing them with goods and services before they have paid for them. Try to get them to recognize this, even if you do it in a light-hearted way. It might help to get them working with you.

In the same way that you should try to get people in accounts departments to work with you rather than against you, remember to call them up and thank them for their help when your payment is shaken loose. It's a bit like remembering to acknowledge good service, rather than just complaining when it's bad. People remember such courtesy and consideration.

Chasing payments from overseas clients

> When it comes to chasing an overseas payment, you are likely to forget quite quickly how exotic and cosmopolitan it felt to be working for that particular client. Tax treaties between different countries can be complex, and I suspect the bureaucracy involved is used by some clients to delay or withhold payment. These can be vexing problems, and it can take a disproportionate amount of time to secure

the payment of a relatively small fee. We have had cases of payments being delayed by five or six months because of supposed local tax regulations. In one instance, we were told our client could not pay until authorized to do so by the German tax authorities. This wasn't just a matter of sending the required paperwork to prove our UK status; we were supposed to believe that payment could not be made to any overseas company without direct permission from the tax authorities. This was too impractical a proposition to be credible, so I eventually spoke to our client's financial controller and told him we would have to contact his client to inform them that since we had not been paid, they were in breach of copyright if they were using the images. The payment came through within 48 hours. Satisfying as this was, it did highlight the difficulties involved in working with overseas companies. The job was for a fairly well-known advertising agency, but I would definitely hesitate before working with them again.

In order to overcome these problems, you can fill in European tax treaty forms that are bi- or trilingual and send them to your local tax office to be stamped, thereby confirming you pay tax in your home country. The forms are valid for a year, and if you complete one for one client in France, it's valid for any other client in France. The problem is that the requirement to have one of these forms in place to avoid losing money on tax withholding is applied arbitrarily, which further convinces me that some clients use the system to delay or reduce payments.

As you can see, there can be a number of problems to overcome if you decide to work in other markets. But if you are prepared to take a few financial and maybe artistic knocks, you can make it work. These risks might be offset by the increase in work opportunities, instead of working for only one market in one economic climate.

Contracts – protecting your rights and yourself

> Contracts are increasingly a daily matter for the freelance illustrator. However, it isn't just a matter of dealing with the ones that are sent to you as part of a new commission; you need to be able to read and understand contracts so that you can put your own terms of business in place for your clients.

Predictably, many contracts are written in seemingly impenetrable language, often referred to as 'legalese', and it's hard to know exactly what the various terms mean, let alone grasp the implications of the clauses themselves. If you can understand the principles, you should be in a better position to state your terms of business in a clear and unequivocal manner, and express your understanding of the contract.

In this respect, the legal aspects of contracts have two sides. The purpose of 'terms and conditions' is to make your clients aware of how you do business, and to express your understanding of the basis on which you are undertaking work. If you put this into plain English, it then forms a kind of agreement, if your client is happy to proceed on that basis.

Alternatively, there are full-blown 'terms and conditions' drawn up by a solicitor that are written in the aforementioned 'legalese'. These outline, in a 'worst case scenario' way, exactly what you are undertaking, what assurances you provide with your services, what you hold the client responsible for, what indemnities you expect and under which legal jurisdiction any dispute would be dealt with. They try to cover every eventuality and, doubtless because of legal precedents, the terms have to be phrased in certain ways. They offer assurances to the client, outlining the limit of any liabilities you are prepared to assume, and are drawn up by a lawyer who will be looking to protect you while not creating 'unreasonable' terms of business.

I have to confess right now that in the early days of running the agency, I had no legally drawn-up terms and conditions in place. After three legal scrapes (which we won), we decided we had to put proper ones in place. One of the cases we won provides a good example of how you can protect your position in a legally defensible way, using your common sense and some clearly articulated understandings.

A salutary lesson

> People will often tell you that you should have all paperwork in place before you do any work, and in an ideal world this would be the case. In reality, work is often needed quite quickly and faster than a company's bureaucracy chooses to operate.

We were working with a small design company on a brochure for a software/bespoke computer-programming company. The illustrator, and I as the agent, were invited to a meeting with the end-user. From the outset, I didn't like the way the project was unfolding. The job was ill-defined by the client, who had no understanding of the services he was buying, while the design company, which I felt should have been guiding and educating the client through the process, was simply letting things drift in an unfocused manner. We were asked to give a 'ballpark' costing based on a very rough outline of what was required. The illustration work was supposed to respond to some 'core principles' that the client had, but these had not yet been written.

As work was being requested immediately, with little in the way of clear guidelines and no purchase order, it seemed prudent to put some parameters in place. I wrote to the client and copied the design company into the letter, which was sent by registered delivery, outlining our understanding of what we were providing and on what basis. Based on the initial ballpark figure, I broke down the cost to a per image fee. Given that there was no decision on how many images would eventually be used, I stated that in the absence of any other understanding, the illustrator's fees would be calculated on a daily rate of £500 ($750) per day, with no licence to use the images. I felt that this way, both client and design company would either focus on what they were doing or rein in what they were asking for. The letter also stated clearly that ownership of the copyright and original artwork rested with the illustrator.

After some three months of work and three months of rambling by the client, the backsliding started. It began with two days of not being able to get the cheque signed because the director was away. Then came the bald demand that the client wanted both the copyright and the original artwork, otherwise 'the director is not going to pay'. Given that it had been repeatedly stated and put in writing that the copyright and artwork were not part of the price, this was a simple attempt to bully us.

I spoke to a lawyer friend, who assessed my paperwork and said I'd made a clear case that could not be contested, so he picked up the phone and told the client to pay within 48 hours or we would bill for the illustrator's time on the stated basis of £500 per day, which would have amounted to more than double the fee being withheld. By the time I got back to the office, there were two indignant faxes of blustering nonsense in response to the lawyer's call. Two hours later, their faxed surrender came through and the payment was biked over the next morning, along with the artwork.

It was a stressful business, but we managed to protect ourselves by stating clearly the terms on which we were supplying our services. Had the client stopped everything on receipt of that letter, the outcome would not have been clear and easy to resolve, but because they continued to request artwork and changes, they were deemed to have accepted those terms. If a situation is not being defined, you can and should make efforts to define it in writing (by e-mail or in a letter) so the basis on which you are supplying your work is clear. By anticipating and addressing potential problems, you can provide yourself with reasonable protection.

Moving on to how to decode contract terminology and terms and conditions, I offer a glossary of certain terms. These are general guidelines only; I am not a lawyer, and the law varies depending on where you are in the world. Just as we have in the past, you will need to obtain your own legal advice regarding any application of this information.

Since writing the first edition of this book, I have unfortunately experienced my artists' copyright being breached, necessitating the involvement of lawyers. The first case ran as anticipated by our legal team. They placed numerous caveats on the anticipated outcome, so had anything come to light that threw doubt on the case, it would have cost us in excess of £50,000 ($75,000). Without good advice it would have been almost impossible to decide whether or not to pursue the case. In the event, the case went forward and we won £200,000 ($300,00). The breach cost the client probably double that, including legal costs. Of course, they could have had a licence for the artwork they used for a fraction of that price.

Another situation should have been an even more clear-cut example of copyright breach. After spending £7000 ($10,500) on preparation of the case and a barrister's assessment (all favourable), we were not able to proceed. The reasons are complicated and partly to do with timing.

The two cases here demonstrate why general legal advice isn't that helpful. Two cases where an equally evident breach of copyright occurred had very different outcomes. If someone does breach your copyright, then good legal advice is essential, whether you address the issue in court or decide to deal with the case yourself. It would not be appropriate for any more precise advice to be given here on matters that are best dealt with by a lawyer.

Glossary

Copyright This is your right of ownership in a piece of work that you have created. Copyright in an image that you have created remains with you unless you physically sign it away by assigning copyright to someone else. This is distinct from the ownership of the physical artwork, in that you can sell an image to someone, say as an original or a print, but this does not include any rights to reproduce that work in any way, without written permission from you. So someone buying your work for their wall can't decide to print a postcard of it and use it as a greeting card.

Licence You can allow someone to reproduce your work by granting them full copyright in the image. Alternatively, and more usually, you do so by granting them specific uses only, over certain periods and in certain territories, with any stipulations you like. In this instance, you are granting a licence to reproduce your work, and the extent of the licence is usually reflected in the fees being paid.

Moral rights This term refers to your right to be identified as the author/creator of your work, but it also covers such things as the right not to have it altered or changed by anyone else. Furthermore, your 'moral rights' in an image mean you have a say in the context in which it appears, so that you can decide whether you and your work are to be associated with whatever that context implies.

Media licences

Outdoor This refers to outdoor posters, train station posters, advertising on the sides of buses or taxis, bus stops and so on.

Press This refers to use of an advertisement in newspapers, both regional and national.

Consumer magazines This refers to use in mainstream or general men's and women's consumer magazines, such as *Esquire*, *GQ*, *Elle*, *Vogue* and *Tatler*.

Trade press This refers to use in trade magazines; trade-specific titles such as *Woodworkers Monthly*.

DM or direct mail This is advertising that comes through the door, in the mail, either stand-alone or along with a piece of related mail from the company whose products or services are being advertised.

PoS or point of sale This can refer to leaflets or postcards available to the public in the stores or branch offices of the end-user client.

Collateral This is a term used in the US rather than in Europe. Advertising agencies talk about buying outdoor, press and web use as well as 'collateral', which seems to be a rounding-up of all the other uses, such as direct mail and point of sale. It's rather convenient for the agency that a few useful media are bundled together, consequently devalued and therefore often underpaid as a media-licence fee.

Buyout If a campaign is expected to be widespread, it's likely that an advertising agency will want a 'buyout' in the use of your image. A buyout refers to use across all media for a given period and in a specified territory. The buyout comes in three categories:

Above the line This refers to advertising usage in the public arena, including appearing on outdoor posters, and in newspapers and consumer magazines. Websites (as opposed to intranet sites, which are limited to company subscribers and not generally accessible by the public) are sometimes considered as 'below the line' uses, but this has changed as web use has become crucial to most campaigns.

Below the line This refers to less obvious locations for the advertising, such as trade magazines, direct mail, point of sale and intranet use.

Through the line A combination of above and below the line. This and the two buyouts described above usually, but not always, exclude television, as it's such a specific usage and tends to be negotiated separately. Some agencies will try to include it in a buyout if it suits their purposes.

Key phrases

> Below is an important piece of text and one that you can put on any invoice or quote you might supply to a client:

Copyright and artwork remain the property of the artist unless otherwise stated. This fee is for the above stated usages only. Any additional usage would need to be negotiated and agreed. All work undertaken is subject to our standard terms and conditions, a copy of which is printed on the reverse. Grant of rights is conditional on payment in full.

To pick apart what this means:

Copyright and artwork remain the property of the artist unless otherwise stated.
For obvious reasons, this is important. Quotations are for particular usages and those usages only. Stating that the copyright remains with the artist reaffirms this basic principle. (In practice, copyright has to be physically assigned, in writing and signed by the artist, but the statement affirms the right to

dictate the extent of the usage.) Stating this is also important because some clients supply purchase orders that have their own terms and conditions printed on the reverse. These sometimes state that any work undertaken for the client becomes the sole property and copyright of the client. Stating clearly that it remains with the artist unless otherwise specified in writing by you does a lot to protect your continued ownership of the copyright.

Stating that the artwork remains the property of the artist confirms that the payment is for the usage licence only and that you, the artist, expect your artwork (where it exists as a physical original artwork) to be returned.

This fee is for the above stated usages only. Any additional usage would need to be negotiated and agreed.
Stating that any usages other than those specified in the quote would need to be negotiated and agreed further emphasizes the limited uses being agreed, and that there would be a fee for any additional uses.

All work undertaken is subject to our standard terms and conditions, a copy of which is printed on the reverse.
This means that the quotation is only part of the deal, and that all terms in the terms and conditions are applicable, both when looking at what the quotation covers and once any work is started. Since the terms and conditions provide much more detail and extensive coverage and protection of rights, this clause is extremely important.

Grant of rights is conditional on payment in full.
This means exactly what it says, that all reproduction and/or usage rights are granted only on the condition that you have been paid in full. The phrase is designed to encourage clients to pay promptly. The reality is that this phrase and your terms and conditions represent a 'hard ball' position, in that if any of this were to go to court, it lays out your maximum level of legal recourse. So, for example, if a client had failed to pay, but had already started using your work, they are effectively in breach of your copyright. This gives you more leverage because legally they could end up paying more than they

originally agreed to pay in fees; they would have to pay your legal costs, and a breach of copyright could mean that anything they have printed would have to be recalled and pulped.

It's an extreme position, but it does prove useful. In the rare instances where my agency has had to take legal action, these are points that focus an errant client's attention.

Where the above discussion leaves you in relation to contracts or terms and conditions issued to you by the commissioning client is open to debate. A lawyer once told me that the last terms and conditions to be issued to either party before commencement of any work are the ones that prevail in the case of a job resulting in legal action by either party. I doubt, somehow, that it is that clear-cut. We operate on the basis that we discuss everything and put it in writing, first as a quotation, then, once any negotiations are concluded, as a confirmation, accompanied by our terms and conditions. The confirmation has to be signed by the client before any work begins. This approach is for design and advertising work, and wouldn't generally be practical for every little editorial or publishing job – for these, we rely on putting the agreed job details into an e-mail, stating that the work is for first, one-time use only in the agreed territory. On seeing any contract the client issues, we raise any objections to any of the clauses as promptly as possible.

I would advise any freelancer to do something similar. In terms of editorial work, discuss the usage and request the contract. Check over what you are about to sign and be prepared to question things. For design and advertising jobs, if you don't have an agent, adopt a similar approach, even if it's a matter of putting your understanding of the job description, intended usage, delivery date and price in a clear and concise e-mail. This way, you can always refer back to the fact that you outlined your understanding of the parameters of the job at the outset, and if someone failed to point out any difference between your understanding and theirs, it's their problem, not yours. You were clear about the basis on which you supplied the work.

To put a disclaimer in here, please remember that I'm not a lawyer, so don't rely on any of the above to cover you legally in the event of a problem. This chapter is intended to offer guidelines and helpful pointers based on my experience, not the last word in copyright law. If you are concerned about a contract, in the first instance you should ask an experienced illustrator for their advice, or approach your local society of illustrators for fuller information on the matter. Ultimately, you may well need to talk to a lawyer for clearer advice and, although that can cost quite a lot of money, it's better to have your facts straight so that you don't get burned if any situation happens to go pear-shaped.

If any contract you're sent is unreasonable and the client will not compromise, you should consider rejecting the commission, as it might be better to avoid setting a bad precedent both for yourself and for other illustrators.

In summary

> Despite all the above – which can sound daunting and make the business of illustration appear terribly adversarial – the fact is that most jobs run smoothly. In the few instances where a rejection occurs, the majority will be dealt with equably enough. If you take note of a few pointers from this chapter, it may just help if you end up with a job that goes wrong. The possibility of this happening certainly needn't dominate your thinking, nor ruin your enjoyment of a very rewarding and, frankly, privileged occupation.

Yuko Shimizu

Can you provide a brief outline of your studies?

> I have a degree in business from Waseda University, Tokyo. After working in corporate PR for 11 years, I moved to New York to enroll in the School of Visual Arts, and did two years of undergraduate illustration studies, then switched to an MFA in Illustration, graduating in 2003.

How well did your studies prepare you for working as an illustrator?

> Two years studying art for the first time gave me the basic skills. Two years of graduate studies taught me how to put my personal voice into my work, and get myself prepared for working freelance.

What were your first experiences of working as an illustrator?

> Every month for about six months I sent self-promotional materials to 30–50 names I wrote down from magazine mastheads at Barnes & Noble bookstore. After six months I started getting work. My first job, around the same time, was for a very small letter section in the *New York Times*, and a spot illustration for the *Village Voice*.

Any memorable incidents from this period?

> I got severely ill while working on my very first colour magazine double-page spread. I was able to get a few days of deadline extension, but I had to work through a severe fever. I had to commute by taxi because I couldn't walk more than a few blocks. This was when I realized the responsibility of being a freelance artist. You have to do everything to finish the job. A huge difference from being an office worker.

How did you cope financially?

> I worked 11 years in a big corporation and saved money. So, after I paid for four years of tuition and groceries, I still had some money left in the bank. I used that to buy time after graduation, spending time working in my studio and creating promotional works till illustration started paying my then very low monthly bill.

Are you methodical in your working life?

> I studied business and I did more than ten years of corporate. I am extremely methodical and organized. I think I write good e-mails, which I believe is very important.

Do you work from home or a studio?

> I work in a studio, which I started immediately after I graduated. Back then, high-speed internet didn't even reach my home area. There was no way I was working from home.

What do you feel are the benefits?

> I was used to corporate life. Although I don't miss it, there are some things I thought worked really well, and one of them was completely separating work and private. I seldom work from home, and it is the clear divide I really like.

Do you have an agent/rep?

> Yes, but we have a very open relationship: we only work together a few times a year when they bring me some advertising-related works, or I get some work that I would rather my agent handled, because it is complicated. Otherwise, 80–90 per cent of the time, I work on my own.

What do you like or dislike about it?

> It is easier when someone experienced is handling advertising work, especially when the client is abroad and business practice differs. Also, some ad agencies only look for illustrators with specific agents. So, there are definitely some jobs I would not have got without my agent.

What kind of promotional activity do you do?

> At first, you need to do a lot of footwork. It gets easier when your work is distributed by itself more and more. Now, the main way to promote my work is through my website. I believe my website is the biggest tool to spread my work out there, and I needed a site that was better than average. Social networking is becoming more and more important. Having a monograph published by a good publisher (Gestalten) has certainly helped. I haven't sent any promotional cards in a few years. My agent does completely different types of promotions to completely different types of clients. And I really need that. If they do the same promotion I do, I don't need them. They promote to places I don't have access to, like ad agencies around the world.

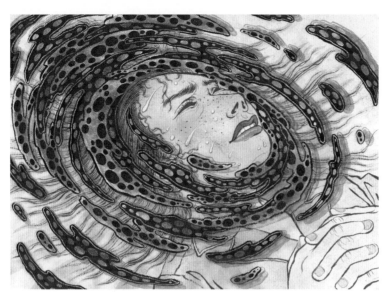

Can you imagine working without an agent?

> I find 80–90 per cent of my work by myself. But that 10 per cent of work, with ad agencies and bigger clients, lets me buy freedom later on, and I really appreciate my agent for that.

Do you have a website?

> I would be really surprised if anyone said no to this question. Then I'd want to know how they are making a living without one.

How does having a website affect your relationship with your agent?

> Their site and my site are completely separate. That is done intentionally to know the source of each assignment, as it affects the way it works and our commissions too.

What social media do you use regularly?

> Facebook. I just started Behance. I do Instagram, but for fun, not for work. A Facebook public page is a good tool, as a post is only distributed to those who have clicked that button to 'like' my work. Announcements for events and website updates go to the right people. I use it more to manage people who are kind enough to like my work, and less to try to get work. I have gotten work on Facebook, but it is just when the art director and I happened to be on FB, so we ended up talking about a project there. I am not sure I would have got the project without Facebook. I am still figuring out social media in that sense.

Has the promotional landscape changed in the last six years?

> Not just the promotional landscape, but everything has changed and keeps changing.

Do you see clients face to face?

> You see people less, you talk to people less. It is the general nature of things. Having said that, it does often help to see people. Human nature doesn't change with the speed of technological advance.

Have you had any bad experiences with clients?

> Who hasn't? It is the nature of life, regardless of which occupation you are in. I have had disputes over payment. I have resolved almost all of them. The only exceptions were when the companies went bankrupt. It only happened a handful of times, and none of them was a huge amount. So I guess I was fortunate in that sense.

Have you ever turned work down for reasons other than not being available?

> I don't take work where I don't believe in the philosophy, or the compensation is too low. My guideline is, if it won't give me a good night's sleep, then that is a job not worth taking.

What do you like most about being an illustrator?

> I do what I love for a living.

What do you like least?

> You end up working all the time.

What do you think is the future of illustration?

> I cannot predict the future, but it is important to diversify, and read the direction in which the world is heading. I am not talking about following the trend here. I mean the general direction of the world determines everything else, and you should be aware of it.

Offer one piece of advice to a new illustrator.

> Life as an illustrator is not easy, but it is so rewarding if you love it. Do it when you love it, so you can go through all the obstacles ahead. But if you don't absolutely love it, then look for something else you will love more. Good luck.

Opposite above: Advertisement for
Tiger Beer
Opposite below: Calendar for *The
Progressive* celebrating interracial marriage,
legalized in the US in 1967
Above left: *Blow Up 3* (personal work)
Above right: *Battle Hymn of Tiger Mother*
(unpublished)
Right: *Fall of a Superwoman* for *Der Spiegel*

Chapter 6
Promoting yourself

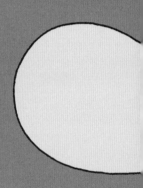

Strategies for	> When approaching self-promotion, it's helpful to start by looking at what you
self-promotion	

Strategies for self-promotion > When approaching self-promotion, it's helpful to start by looking at what you want to achieve. Asking yourself such a fundamental question can help focus your approach. In basic terms, it's about getting work and then keeping a flow of work coming to you, hopefully much of which will be repeat business from clients who become semi-regulars. Before you decide how you promote, you need to look at exactly *who* you promote to.

In discussing how to get your first job, we looked at the very basic means of finding out who to contact. As you gear up your self-promotional engines, you need to develop a methodical and structured approach to keeping that information up to date and to expanding your list of would-be clients. In this respect, your database maintenance will dovetail with your promotional activity by necessity.

The stages and requirements of self-promotion probably divide into three categories. The first brings you initial contact with, and work from, a client. This includes their viewing your portfolio and subsequently being commissioned by them.

The second is concerned with how you keep in contact with the people you've seen or worked with, or who have expressed interest in working with you. You need to think about how to stay close to the forefront of their minds, without making a nuisance of yourself.

The third category of self-promotion is general profile-raising. This is not immediately quantifiable in terms of success rate versus time, energy and money spent. You are not looking to this kind of promotion to bring you calls from clients or work directly. It's the more oblique approach, which can enhance your reputation and also raise your stock. This area of self-promotion has been enhanced by the advent of social media and the explosion of related activity.

All these facets can blend seamlessly together and may overlap, but you need to consider their different aims so that you can plan a strategy of sorts, to keep up a steady flow of activity that addresses them all. You can then start to look at which options are open to you and which to choose for the different aspects of self-promotion you wish to cover.

Websites > Most illustrators seem to have a website by the time they leave college, and this can certainly be a great tool in your promotional armoury. You should look upon your site as the basic foundation of your self-promotion. That said, you do need to look carefully at what function it fulfils.

Is it an online sketchbook, where you can make it a playground for your experimental work, with bits of animation and quirky click-me icons to lead the visitor through it? Or is it an online portfolio, simply showcasing your best pieces of work in a straightforward fashion?

Websites are the number one innovation in self-promotion. They are affordable – you can build one yourself if you are so inclined, or you can get an 'architect' in and create a really elegant, sophisticated site that loads swiftly, is easy to navigate and quickly gets the visitor to where they want to be. Whichever route you choose, don't forget the website's function, and keep that as a focus. If it is designed to be a showcase of your best work that clients can browse through with a view to commissioning you, you need to ensure they can get to this online portfolio promptly, without flailing around in an ill-considered navigational system that takes ages to load. Provide the fast route and the scenic route if need be, ensuring both are well signposted. At least that way you'll have given clients the choice. Ensure that any visitors have quick, direct and clear access to your contact details. It's obvious, but it can get overlooked.

In addition to thinking through the functions you want your website to perform, do some research on how other people's sites are organized. Look at the websites of other illustrators, both students and relative newcomers, as well as bigger, well-established names. Note what you think works and what doesn't. Even established illustrators can get their website architecture wrong. Looking at a wide selection of other sites will help you determine what is most appropriate for you and your profile.

'An experimental site can be fine as long as it doesn't get in the way. Speed, simplicity and large images work best; common irritants are slowness, confusing navigation, and intro screens or sequences.'

Luke Hayman,
Pentagram, New York

The quote from Luke Hayman (left) holds true and is a good barometer of the patience of your potential clients. It's about staying focused on a clear goal and message and being as concise as possible. Art directors are busy people, so you need to cut to the point promptly.

Having a website is fine, but getting the people you want to see it looking at it, and generally directing traffic to it, are crucial. Without visitors, your site is out in the wilderness. Links can help here. It's good to include links to other interesting websites. It results in higher ratings with search engines, so that your site comes up higher in any search results, but it also helps in establishing what kind of artist you are. You can add links to things you've found and liked and think your visitors might get a kick out of. This provides a kind of context for you and your work. I wouldn't go so far as to say the links that you offer define you, but they do help build a picture of you as a creative individual. This linking of individuals and sites is also the fuel for such sites as LinkedIn and Facebook. It appears to be a serendipitous approach to networking, one which may make traditional networking seem rather quaint, but both have a role to play.

Equally, of course, you want other people to put a link to your site on theirs. This can be a bit more difficult to control, as you need people to do this because they want to. Setting up reciprocal links with friends can be a good start. Thereafter, I suspect it's a case of viral marketing; if your particular content is sufficiently interesting, it will pass by 'word of mouse' through the great global network.

There are limitations to the value of this kind of networking – certainly if you're relying on it alone to bring in work. The limitations that spring to mind are the same as with any website of undefined purpose. A potential client can browse online in the hope of stumbling across something interesting that they can use, but the majority are unlikely to have the time or patience.

Certainly, there are creatives who will be happy to browse in the hope of finding fresh talent to bring to their commercial practice. However, the percentage of clients searching in this way is likely to be quite small, and therefore your chances of getting regular work on the strength of such promotion is equally limited. I suspect that another underlying problem with this kind of approach is the potential to be a one-hit wonder, a lucky find, used and then forgotten in the search for something newer and more interesting.

The other danger is not knowing the value of your work or the credentials of anyone you may end up dealing with. However, if this kind of networking is done in conjunction with more traditional approaches, it can potentially add the spice of chance and serendipity to who might contact you, impressed with your work.

If you use a blog to promote your work, be aware of the impression comments and chatter can create. Lots of in-jokes between friends can leave someone looking at your work from a professional perspective cold and unimpressed. In short, think about your target audience, not just about yourself.

Postcards > Don't overlook the printed postcard as a reliable tool for self-promotion. It can seem a rather dull option, but consider it a promotional workhorse, solid and reliable. Not only is it a useful calling card, which can feature one or more images plus your contact details, but also it can direct people to your website.

The 'death of print', although much talked about, is much like any other prophecy – inaccurate, if not outright nonsense. Years ago, the paperless office was hailed as the way forward, but the amount of paperwork that pours through the door daily and is generated by printing hard copies means there is probably more, not less, paper in the office than ever before. If you go to see a client for that precious face-to-face meeting where you are given the opportunity to show your work and talk about it, you need something to leave behind.

It needs to be something that holds the client's attention and represents exactly what you do. If you can afford full-colour printing on both sides of a card, I'd suggest one full-size image on one side with two or three smaller ones on the reverse. It depends on the images, but there is no point squeezing in too many if you can't see much at such a reduced scale. A certain amount of 'flavour' can be conveyed, though, and this can be enough to draw the intrigued towards your website for a proper browse through your portfolio.

Sometimes, adding some brief text is beneficial. If you can convey fairly concisely what it is you do, and why you do it that way, in an interesting manner, it's a bonus. A brief client list is also useful. Whatever text you decide to put on your card, make sure it's well designed. This will ensure that a lot of information can be included, and that the card will still feel spacious and uncluttered. A poorly designed card can seriously undermine your work. Presentation is everything to those in the business of presentation.

A selection of promotional delights from Jonny Hannah's Cakes and Ale Press

Assuming you have a website, a postcard could be used and seen as your 'pre-homepage'. It's the tool that will guide people to your site so they can check out the rest of your work.

Sarah Thomson

Art Buyer, Fallon, London

When did you first work with an illustrator?

> I commissioned a campaign illustrating children and animals at AMV. It was very good experience but I don't think it ran in the end!

When do you call on the services of illustration?

> Frequently — when an idea has been conceived as an illustration or it suits that idea best; when we need something unusual, different or individual; sometimes when budgets or branding are issues.

Do you have a stable of illustrators you turn to often?

> Yes and no. There are some we use frequently, as they are always brilliant. They do a wonderful job, on time, and are lovely to work with — but we only use them when they're absolutely right for a job; just as often we use illustrators we haven't commissioned before.

Where do you look for talent?

> Magazines, newspapers, e-mails, websites, annuals, books, meetings with artists and agents.

What do you feel are illustration's strengths?

> There is a huge variety of styles to choose from, and a style can become synonymous with a particular client. It's versatile in application and can be very accessible, charming, direct and appealing to its audience.

Why choose it over alternatives?

> It's very individual. If reality's not an issue, the idea is often best conveyed by illustration.

Have you found illustrators are open to art direction?

> Almost all are open to it; it seems many like the collaboration.

How do you feel about cropping or adjusting artwork?

> In a commercial environment, it could happen. Images need to be adapted to suit varying magazine sizes. If work needs to be adjusted, the illustrator should be given the first opportunity to do so; if that's not possible, we would always try and get changes to them for approval. It may also depend on work being on brief and of the standard required.

What kind of promotional items work best for you?

> Cards are increasingly un-green but still a useful work tool, as are e-mails with links to websites and recent work. We often attend exhibitions to which we're invited. Large printed pieces can be tricky as they are difficult to display.

When do you decide to see someone with their portfolio?

> I generally ask to see examples of work from a website or as jpegs first. But it's more memorable to meet face to face.

Given the ease of viewing images online, do you still see artists with their portfolios?

> If you meet people in person, it can make a strong impression and a memorable meeting, which is good for me — especially if I like the work! — and good for the artist, too.

How do you choose who to see?

> If their work is really unsuited to our clients, then I would decline seeing someone. When I have appointments booked for more than about three months ahead I don't see people, but this isn't generally the rule. It's important for me to see artists.

What do you like to see in a paper portfolio?

> If the portfolio is an exact replica of the website or vice versa, it's not as useful. But in some cases just gearing the portfolio carefully to each medium can be enough.

What do you look for?

> Brilliant imagery, presented with care. A good portfolio is really important. If you're unfamiliar with work, then they are a very accessible way of seeing it in the best light, concentrating on it fully.

Do you have any pet hates?

> Those huge old art cases with scratched plastic sleeves that have all broken so pages fall out when you turn them over and then you can't do them up again!

Do you source artists via social media sites?

> Not really, or not exclusively, but they are sometimes part of the platform from which we view work.

What would be your advice to a new, would-be illustrator?

> Be open-minded. An apparently lowly job has potential to be great. Treat everyone with respect; juniors could be creative directors one day! Keep your portfolio updated and looking fantastic. Be flexible and expect the unexpected; things can change during any job for myriad reasons.

E-mail **>** As well as being a major innovation for illustrators promoting themselves, the internet provides a platform on which they can display their work, and can provide access to a larger market, irrespective of location. E-mail enables you to put you and your message in front of your desired audience – provided you have the appropriate addresses. However, what differentiates your message and attached 'sample' from spam? Being unsolicited, they could be about as welcome. So, if you are going to promote yourself via e-mail, tread carefully and work out how to make sure your message is welcomed rather than considered a nuisance. By thinking about your recipient, you can make yourself stand out from those who blithely send samples by e-mail without asking first.

Again, put yourself in the shoes of a busy art director whose inbox keeps filling up with unsolicited e-mails and attachments. To send such samples and a long rambling autobiography to someone who never asked for them is like walking up to a stranger in the street, talking about yourself and trying to show him or her some pictures you made. Go back to basic interpersonal skills and think about it.

Try a simple and concise message that asks how the intended recipient would prefer to see samples – by e-mail or as printed images. Once someone has answered that question, if they are happy to receive some samples by e-mail your message is no longer spam. We've found a little consideration goes a long way. In the digital age it's useful to remember you are still dealing with flesh-and-blood individuals.

E-mailing images to multiple recipients is a very efficient and inexpensive means of marketing your work in a targeted way. You can monitor the response to your mailings via software programmes that allow you to see what interest levels you are achieving. As an agency, Heart now uses MailChimp to send out bulk e-mailings to carefully selected client lists. This service provides access to response statistics, so you can see the number of people opening and viewing the mail and the numbers who go further and click on the included links to websites. It's very revealing and the response levels fluctuate a surprising amount.

E-mail dos and don'ts **>** Don't send a collection of samples by e-mail without asking first.

Do write a short, succinct and polite e-mail introducing yourself, saying where you graduated (and when, perhaps) and asking if they would be kind enough to look at some samples of your work via a URL. Include your contact details.

Do send a full URL to a website or Flickr page, or some other direct way of viewing your work quickly with the minimum of navigational fuss or pop-ups.

Don't write a lengthy e-mail, sharing your thoughts on your work. It's a major presumption that your recipient wants to know.

Don't ask for feedback. If people like the work, they will tell you. Asking is just another demand on the time of a busy stranger.

Do remember you are not the only person contacting this particular source of work. Don't be over-confident because you're contacting someone remotely. So many art buyers do the job because they enjoy working with someone on a personal level. If they find you objectionable, it's unlikely they'll bother working with you. There are plenty of illustrators to choose from.

Annuals > Annuals are big commercial catalogues that you can pay to appear in, such as *Contact*, *Le Book* and *American Showcase*, to name but a few. It costs a set amount of money for a set amount of space, and you choose which pieces of work you want printed. These annuals sell themselves on the basis that they are distributed free to a set number of designers and art directors, and that you will recoup your expenditure several times over during the course of the year.

There are no real specializations in the annuals that I'm aware of. All types of illustration are to be found within their covers. If you can pay for space, you're in, so there is no editing process; and if you take a single page, you have no say in whether it is left hand or right hand, or in what goes on the opposite page. If you get an eyesore opposite your work, that's just the luck of the draw.

Submission, production, publishing and distribution dates for annuals vary. There is no one time of the year when they all come out. Consequently, in planning the following year's promotion, you can decide when you want it to appear. Some annuals begin distribution in January, and some in March or April. This is something you'll need to check out locally. However, there's no reason why you can't consider running a page in an annual published overseas.

Choosing images for annuals is similar to choosing them for a postcard. If you are doing several different kinds of printed promotion, you have to strike a balance between using your favourite or strongest pieces and the danger inherent in using the same image (or images) repeatedly. If you have a 'signature' image that you want to use, balance it with some variation in the accompanying ones. There's a fine line between reinforcing your message and becoming repetitive. If you use an annual more than once, you'll hopefully have a new signature image. If not, you risk looking like a one-trick pony.

Annuals work to a degree but you remain one among hundreds, if not thousands, of illustrators. Advertising agencies do seem to use them quite a lot. Since art buyers are often asked to call in portfolios of a certain style, annuals are ideal tools for them to flick through. Annuals usually have accompanying websites; sometimes inclusion on these sites is included in the fee for your space in the book, sometimes it will involve a supplementary fee. Such sites generally provide live links to your own website or e-mail, or both. Doubtless the website element is a useful accompaniment to the annual, but for recipients of these books the flick factor can sometimes outdo the click factor.

Competition annuals > These, as the name suggests, are competitive and not merely a matter of paying the appropriate fee for inclusion. An annual's usefulness as a promotional tool depends on how favourably it is looked upon by commissioning designers and art directors. While the various competition annuals don't specialize, they are likely to be known for favouring certain kinds of work. They are not 'closed shops', reserved only for one genre of work, but their judging panels are often known to favour particular approaches, either more maverick or more traditional illustration.

On this basis, competition annuals tend to have reputations that they work either to maintain or to overcome. If a competition or society annual has had a poor reputation for a long time, it can take years to change people's perception of it. You only need to ask a few illustrators to get a feel for the reputation of a given annual and how its content is regarded by the creative community.

Submission and publication dates for competition annuals vary, so you need to make enquiries in order to get work ready in time if you want to submit your work. If you don't think ahead on this, you might miss a deadline by just a couple of weeks. Because of the lead times involved in judging and production, this could mean your work won't have any chance of appearing in that annual for at least another 18 months.

There is an editing process in place with competitive annuals, in that work is viewed and judged by your peers and/or commissioners as being fit or unfit for inclusion. This might suggest that those commissioning prefer to look at the best examples of illustration work out there. This notion has to be offset by the possibility that their options are more limited and they are choosing from work selected by someone else. If the reputation of the judges or the body holding the competition is not held in high regard, this in turn will reduce the value of the annual.

The reputations of the various competitive annuals wax and wane, with one or two maintaining a consistently high reputation. The costs for these books are generally less than the straightforward commercial annuals. Aside from the issue of getting selected, you have to cover the submission fees plus the print costs for your piece or pieces to appear in the book. These can rack up, but should still end up costing significantly less than in the commercial annuals. You will also have the satisfaction of having been judged worthy by your peers.

Each job acts as an ad > Each job that you do acts as an advertisement for you and your work. The somewhat hackneyed plea from some clients that a poorly paid job would nevertheless be good for raising your profile stems directly from this. There's obviously a degree of truth in what they say, even if it is a bit lame, and a rather cheap selling point for a job that pays a lot less than it ought to. However, work you do that appears in the national press and consumer magazines definitely generates more work. Art directors will always be looking at magazines put out by other publishers and illustrations used in their daily paper. If a magazine runs a particularly well-known column that regularly uses illustrators, the chances are it will be checked out just as regularly. My own second illustration commission was for just such a column, in *The Observer* newspaper. Each illustrator was given the job for four weeks in a row, so it was a good chance to show what you could do. I had an exponentially increasing number of calls for work that came directly from clients seeing my illustrations for that column. If something catches a designer's or art director's eye, they'll note who it's been done by and track that individual down. Work tends to generate work; the more you do, the more you'll get asked to do. This holds as true for well-established illustrators as for those who are just starting out.

Global marketing   > Beyond the ability to disseminate your promotional message to people, e-mail allows you to send artwork across huge distances and almost instantaneously. What this means is that, language barriers notwithstanding, you can work for anyone anywhere, if they are online. This creates a global market for the illustrator as a 'small supplier'. However, it all comes down to interpersonal skills, cultural differences, time differences and establishing relationships. You can be online, but if you have lousy interpersonal skills, then (unless you are a world-class genius) it isn't going to do you much good – most art directors are too busy to massage oversized egos.

When I decided to set up a sister agency to Heart in New York, it stemmed partly from the enjoyment of visiting the city (and thus having a better excuse to go there) and partly from the desire to extend our 'fishing grounds'. If e-mail and a website had solved all the issues, we'd be in London, pitching our work from there. It's more convenient and less expensive, but again the bottom line was about being there, only a local phone call away from clients and potential clients, in the same time zone and building relationships. You have to plug in culturally, too. If you are looking to get into advertising work, to an extent it's going to be dependent on your ability to cross cultural divides. This arguably starts with appearing in editorial contexts and building the presence of your work.

However, if your work isn't any different from what's already available locally, why would anyone choose to commission you from a few thousand miles away? The so-called technological revolution has brought great innovations to our industry, but don't forget the human factor – it is the difference between getting people interested and making them yawn or be downright irritated.

Another consequence of the global marketplace is that, technically, you can work from anywhere. Recently, one of our artists took off to India for six weeks of drawing on location. Without carrying a laptop, he managed to deliver work for two regular slots to clients in London and New York. He did it by means of internet cafés and fax bureaus that offered scanning and e-mailing services. Where there's a will, there is usually a way.

Extracurricular   > These are an extension of promotional activity and, at the same time, can
activities   potentially be an extension of your business and generate income. Many artists I know, and certainly most of those we represent as an agency, generate pieces

that are not produced for commissioned jobs. This is arguably part of one's professional practice, in that it's wise to renew, develop and refine the work upon which your business is built.

Once a career is established, you can find yourself jumping relentlessly from one job to the next, with a huge proportion of your time spent working. Since you can be overwhelmed by the demands of pressing deadlines, many running concurrently, the motivation to set aside time for extra work can easily dissipate. Over and above handling the incoming jobs and deadlines, you have all the other aspects of your business to deal with: billing, chasing payments, paying bills, sorting out promotion, maintaining databases and so on. Finding the time, energy and discipline to produce more work at your own bidding can be a tall order.

You may well find that many clients commission on the strength of the same one or two pieces of work. It can initially be very gratifying to know that those particular illustrations are so universally liked, and that you got something right with them. The problem is, when people commission on the basis of a certain piece, they often want a variation of that artwork, adjusted to their subject matter. This might work once or twice, but you may well find yourself doing forced reworkings of the same piece, rather than developing and moving forward. Finding time to develop your work outside the commercial arena is therefore essential.

Social media networks > Before signing up to every social media network, it is worth looking at how they function and considering how they can be used in self-promotion. Much like the arrival of e-mail and websites, social media has been surrounded by so much opinion, it's often hard to separate the hard reality from the hype.

Illustrator Marion Deuchars says that she uses Facebook, Twitter, Pinterest and Statigram, although only when she has something specific to promote. She has used these networks to generate interest in and sales of her books, but seemed less able to quantify their value as direct promotional tools for her illustration work.

'At the moment, it's the only strategy I have. Print/post, telephone calls, seeing people (including travelling time) are not efficient or eco-friendly, and also expensive. It's hard to prove the value in terms of response.

'However, in my case, what I find interesting is the opportunity to reach a new and often younger audience, which would be harder without social media. Also, I don't babble on social media. When I have something interesting to say or show (about my work), I blog, tweet etc. That might be once a week or once a month.

'But you have to promote, so promote in whatever means are relevant to the time. There is no measure apart from, in my case, sale of books, or getting continual work. Companies advertise and look at sales figures to see results. Sometimes the advertising works in a different way and is not always translatable into sales. However, like most companies, mine included, not to advertise is foolhardy.'

There are a number of caveats to consider in Marion's case. She is not a newcomer to the world of illustration. She has a well-established reputation and audience, who are receptive to her selective promotion of work via social media. The same approach may not work on its own for a relative newcomer.

The online networks of links and connections between people seem to work on the basis of 'six degrees of separation': nobody is separated from anyone, anywhere, by more than six connections. A colleague tells me of a second-year graphics student who has a phenomenal site with links to dozens of companies and key individuals in the music and promotion business. Furthermore, he describes the phenomenon of self-created celebrity; video clips of this student being 'interviewed' by a friend are on YouTube. The interview provides a vehicle for the student to create the impression that her views on art, design, music and youth culture are highly regarded. Whether or not this is true, YouTube has certainly provided a platform for the student's views, and her music and club-night flyers and T-shirts have developed into quite a presence, resulting in an advertising creative finding her work and commissioning her for a campaign. Doubtless there are hundreds of others out there, creating a similar kind of hype that generates interest in their work from unpredictable sources. This connectivity has the potential to create a wave of interest in your work.

In an age when you can follow a fishfinger on Facebook and Twitter, you need to think seriously about how you differentiate yourself from the social media noise, in order to create interest that becomes a following. A following gets you talked about, and then someone in a position to commission you might notice you.

I am a little cynical about this, mainly because I doubt I will ever want to look at the Facebook page of a fishfinger. That aside, social media can obviously have a huge chatter impact on self-promotion. Much as with websites, it's about getting attention, and then directing it. It's also about harnessing this potential alongside many other modes of self-promotion, to create an orchestrated strategy.

I'm still struck by the core issue that be it a website, a blog, a Facebook page or a Twitter presence, it remains a matter of how you get attention or traffic. Some bloggers and tweeters are chatting into the void, which as a promotional activity is pointless. There is a blizzard of activity out there, and you are potentially one voice trying to be heard among thousands.

Blogs can act as a useful archive and are easy to update, but, as above, they need traffic. What drives the traffic? New York-based artist Yuko Shimizu said she thought it was unwise to rely too heavily on any one social media network because they go out of fashion very quickly.

'All social media (at least up to this point) have a relatively short lifespan. Don't build your world inside a medium that is in its prime now, as you may have to switch over all you have built up to a new medium, which will have its own lifespan. For example, I think that having a blog on Blogger is starting to look very dated. People laugh at you if you still have a MySpace account. A website is something you own and have total control over. Of course, every now and then you have to update the way it looks, but still it is yours, and it will be safe as long as you run and own your domain and hosting. Besides, social media, at least at this point, can never be a substitute for a website.

'My main way to promote my work is through my website. I spent a lot of time and money to get my website rebuilt this year by a very experienced, skilled studio who understood my vision. It was not a small investment, but I believe my website is the biggest tool to spread my work out there.'

Interestingly, although she uses Facebook, Behance and Instagram for example, Yuko couldn't say precisely why social media works or if it was quantifiable. It was more a sense of needing to be part of the conversation.

'We can go on and on about social media, but as an instructor [at SVA in New York City] who teaches a younger generation of artists, my simple answer is this: These kids know about social media and how to use it way more than we do. I am the one who has to constantly think and strategize. They manoeuvre it very intuitively. After all, they are the generation who had blogs since middle school, and they don't remember not having e-mail or text messaging.'

Yuko offered another tip. 'Don't make your fan page too early. Nothing is sadder than a fan page that's been sitting on a site for a while and has only 25 fans. They are likely to be your best friends and family members. You are doing this to make yourself look good, and that just makes you look sad. There are other ways of promoting your work on social media.

'Can you clearly see the return in terms of work brought in by it? Not really. You do need to work constantly on multiple marketing tools (my agent does different promotional things too), and often it is the combination that works. The equation is not that simple.'

In essence, while the social media networks provide a multitude of different ways in which to broadcast your work, the result is essentially just that, a broad cast. It's casting work out into the online world and allowing serendipity to play a part. In terms of a strategic approach to promotion, the social media networks provide a great way to make your work part of a bigger conversation and create direction-finding signals for your website, which should still be considered your primary promotional tool.

Self-motivation > Before I paint too bleak a picture of artistic drudgery, let's be realistic. You are paid for doing something you enjoy, so a healthy degree of self-motivation ought to remain. I just want to point out that, from the outside, being an illustrator can seem rosier than it really is. Everybody needs to do something different occasionally, and deadlines aren't tame in terms of your being able to control when they fall. So, renewing your visual batteries has to be factored into your busy working life, as well as into any other form of life you might want to have.

A strong motivating factor is often the build-up of frustration at small compromises made while working to someone else's brief. Requests for changes in colour, the dropping of a detail, the addition of an unnecessarily clumsy visual 'clue' to ram home the link between image and story can make an illustrator long for the opportunity to do some unadulterated picture-making. Opportunities where all the decisions about the image are yours and yours alone can take various forms.

Self-initiated projects on a theme of particular interest to you are a good starting point. You may have an obsessive interest in something that you want to build a series of artworks around, or it can be as simple as a series of works based on a book you've been reading – almost anything, in fact.

The initial motivation can falter quite quickly in the face of other work pressures, but this depends on your personality type and how disciplined you are. I've never been very self-disciplined, so the fixed deadlines involved in illustration are ideal. In a college environment, I often found prompt, clear decision-making difficult and was always prone to procrastination. Since then, I've learned that I work best under pressure and generally quite fast – too fast to put things off, in fact. This works well with deadlines, but a self-initiated project could allow me to procrastinate. Now, when I am doing anything I could get out of, or that offers me too many excuses for not doing it, I create a deadline that will be enforced by outside factors that I can't sidestep. So, if you're planning a self-initiated project to create a series of artworks, I suggest you introduce a deadline, so that you have a time limit and an amount of work to produce within that span of time. If you are intending to produce a body of work, you can post it on your website or include it in your portfolio, but you could also plan an exhibition around it.

Exhibiting your work   > An exhibition of your work, whether it's to showcase existing illustrations and new pieces, or just to showcase a purpose-made, self-initiated body of work, can perform several functions. Given the aforementioned problem of self-discipline, booking an exhibition space for an as yet uncreated body of work is a very strong motivator in getting you to commit time and energy to a self-initiated project.

Having an exhibition will also provide you with an opportunity to generate PR for yourself. Getting clients and would-be clients along to a show allows you to meet them in a more sociable and relaxed environment. Admittedly, you may not be quite so relaxed since it's your show, but once the work is done and mounted on walls, a certain fatalism takes over, and it either goes down well or it doesn't. You've met the deadline, so that particular game is over.

If you feel too intimidated by the idea of a solo exhibition, you can go for a two-person show or a group show. A two-person show means you can spur each other along, and it's possibly more fun when two people exhibit together. There are twice as many reasons for clients to come along and costs can be shared. Remember, though, that a two-person show can become fractious if one person's work goes down better than the other's – it happens, and you need to acknowledge the possibility from the outset.

The alternative is a group show with three or more of you. There's arguably more potential for creating a buzz around a group show of new talent, although that depends on how you go about promotion. There are even more reasons for would-be clients to come to the show, as they can see a range of work by different artists. If you opt for a group show, it is arguably a bigger draw for some clients – but equally, their attention is divided. You will be relying on a group buzz to carry the show, and sharing in the pay-off. A solo show requires more courage maybe, but potential pay-offs are bigger, as are the risks – both financial and to your reputation. The risk is what makes an exhibition such a powerful motivator.

An exhibition creates an outlet for self-initiated work. It provides opportunities to meet and greet clients in a convivial atmosphere, and can raise your profile as a hot commodity on the illustration market. Another fringe benefit is the potential to raise money by selling work, which can help offset the costs of the show.

A good exhibition party will increase the likelihood that you and your work are remembered. Much depends on the kind of illustrations you exhibit, how well the show is organized and put together, the choice of venue, how it is promoted and who goes to it. If you do it well, it will increase your status as an artist and boost your unique selling point. The more distinctive your USP, the greater your currency within the illustration industry. People will value your work differently and may be prepared to consider paying more for your services.

Self-publishing

> An alternative outlet for self-initiated work is self-publishing. Some artists are particularly drawn to this, most obviously those interested in narrative (often in the form of graphic novels or cartoons). Again, these books can be individual efforts or they can incorporate the work of other artists.

'Self-publishing gives you more freedom, but more responsibility to your audience, so you need to be art director, editor and client as well as artist.'

Tom Gauld, Illustrator

The first consideration in self-publishing is cost of production and whether you physically produce the books yourself or have them printed and bound by someone else. If you can afford your chosen method of production, then you have to think about distribution. Does the self-publishing venture depend on sales to recoup costs, or is it intended as a freely distributed piece of self-promotion, that earns its keep by bringing in work? Whichever it is, there are many options for low-cost production, without too many compromises on quality.

If you opt for 'cottage industry' publishing using a photocopier, your costs can't get much lower. To boost quality, choose a better-than-average paper stock. Beyond that, pay attention to details, so that the copies are as pristine as possible (if that's what you are aiming for); check for dust specks and dirt on the copier and make sure the toner is being laid down evenly. All basic mechanical points, but details can be everything. Alternatively, if you are not good on fine details, choose an approach that has a more *ad hoc* quality. Provided something is supposed to look messy or off-square, it's not a problem. If something that's supposed to look square on the page is trimmed sloppily, it will scream out and ruin the presentation of the work.

Victo Ngai

Opposite left: *Sweet Dreams* for *The New Yorker*
Opposite right: *Casserole* for *The New Yorker*
Below: *Utopia*

Victo (Victoria) Ngai is a New York based illustrator, recently graduated, who uses social media.

Can you provide a brief outline of your studies?

> I graduated from Rhode Island School of Design (RISD) with a BFA in Illustration.

How well did your studies prepare you for working as an illustrator?

> I owe my career to my portfolio teacher Chris Buzelli. Having the fortune to study with him not only helped me develop the conceptual and stylistic chops, it also taught me how the business works (contracts, copyright, client relationships etc.). Chris has also opened many doors by introducing me to great mentors, such as Yuko Shimizu.

What were your first experiences of working as an illustrator?

> Chris Buzelli's wife is the creative director SooJin Buzelli of *Plansponsor*, *Planadviser* and *aiCIO* magazines. During junior year of college, Chris brought in a *Plansponsor* assignment and told our class that the best piece could get published. The assignment smoothed my transition between college and the real world. By the time I graduated, I already had a portfolio of professional work.

Any memorable incidents from this period?

> An illustrator friend asked me, 'How come you get to draw animals and I get assignments with businessmen in suits?' I was taught that the best works are honest works, so I built a portfolio with images that interest me (although they were mostly for trade magazines). This portfolio helped me build a pool of clients who appreciate my 'unconventional' problem solving. I am often asked by students if they should tailor their portfolio for clients. I think it's good to an extent to show that you have an understanding of the publications and are sincere about the jobs, but it's important to make sure what you sell is what you love to do.

How did you cope financially?

> My roommate and I found a cheap apartment in Brooklyn and we lived pretty frugally. I was also lucky to have a couple of fantastic clients by the time I graduated, including SooJin and the *New York Times*. This allowed me to focus on my illustration career without having to take part-time jobs.

Do you work from home or a studio?

> Home.

Do you have an agent/rep?

> Yes, I am represented by Morgan Gaynin, Inc.

What do you like or dislike about it?

> The biggest benefit of having a rep is that I can focus on making art while they do the money talk for me: negotiating contracts and rates, selling me for potential projects, chasing payments etc.

What kind of promotional activity do you do?

> My agent sends out mailer and e-mailer blasts for me. We both promote via social media. For the handful of 'dream clients', I target them by mailing them personal notes, cold-calling for portfolio reviews and introducing myself (shamelessly) to them at illustration events and openings. I also enter major competitions, which proved to be a pretty effective promotional tool as well.

Do you have a website?

> Yes. It serves as a professional portfolio that allows people to check out my work any time. It's also a hub that links to my other sites, such as Twitter, Tumblr etc.

What social media do you use regularly?

> Facebook, Twitter, Tumblr, Behance and Drawger. I think the internet makes promotion

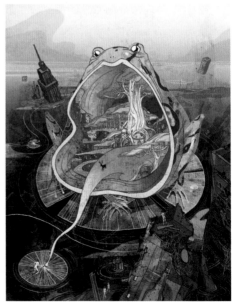

a two-way street. It's great to be proactive and reach out with conventional promos like mailers but it's even better if clients are able to discover me. Social media has the ultimate snowball effect. Through reblogs and retweets, my work can be spread to the most unexpected places.

Is social media important in promoting your work?

> A couple of examples of how I have benefited from internet exposure. I was invited to participate in an art fair at Somerset House in London, which led to my prints being purchased by the Victoria and Albert Museum store. I was interviewed for the 'Innovators' programme on a leading Bulgarian radio station. These are opportunities that I didn't know existed before.

Can you clearly see a return?

> Yes, my first big ad job came through the net. Leo Burnett was scouting out illustrators online for the McDonald's Dragon New Year poster, they contacted me after seeing my portfolio on Behance.

Also, I sell limited-edition giclee prints of my illustrations, making up about a third of my annual income. Gaining a big following online has helped the sales a lot.

How important is social media in your promotional armoury, and why?

> Social media plays a very important role, but other promotions are equally important. I see promotions as branding campaigns: any effective means to get my art out there is valid, as I can never anticipate where jobs come from. Also, as great as social media is, it's still no match for the personal connections I was able to establish with my clients. There are so many talented illustrators for an assignment. I think who gets the job depends on who comes to the art director's mind first. With a face attached to the work, the impression an illustrator has on an art director is much stronger.

Do you think the promotional landscape is changing?

> Fewer and fewer publications

are still doing portfolio drop offs or reviews. Also, more and more people, including art directors, are against printed promos due to environmental concerns. The internet will play a more and more important role in promotion.

What do you like most about being an illustrator?

> Making a living from what I love to do, and the freedom of working anywhere and at any time.

What do you like least?

> Freelance illustration is more than a career – it's a lifestyle. Sometimes it becomes impossible to separate work and personal life. I often have to cancel plans because of rush jobs. Also, without any official office hours, it's very easy to overwork. The worst part is, an artist's work is the product of their thought processes, habits, taste and preferences, which makes it difficult not to take things personally when I have a bad work day.

What do you think is the future of illustration?

> From tapestries to tablets, the media may change but I think illustration will always be around.

Offer one piece of advice to a new illustrator.

> The ones who eventually make it are not necessarily the most talented ones but the most persistent ones.

There are many small printers out there who are friendly, interested, helpful and up for doing something a bit unusual. Cheap black-and-white litho printing is an option, but it's obviously not going to be as low-cost as the trusty photocopier.

A wealth of small bookshops sell low-run or limited-edition books. There are also a lot of specialist art and design stores that stock self-published titles, although, ultimately, these have to be interesting enough for the shop to want to stock them. You can also, of course, sell your wares via your website.

Many of your potential clients are out to charge their creative batteries by checking what is going on out there, and such specialist bookshops with their 'guerrilla' published items are popular browsing places. Clients who stumble across something new may well approach you about a job very differently from how they might approach you if you had bombarded them with standard promotional items. And they may feel a little more personal satisfaction in having discovered you themselves.

A small book from Tom Gauld's Cabanon Press

If you make such bespoke, self-published items but aren't interested in selling them, mailing them to your clients can work well. A book is different from and more memorable than the average 'promo' material they receive. Ventures into self-publishing and book design also provide an opportunity to exercise your work on the page, on the cover and perhaps with type – to show how you would ideally like your illustrations to be seen. In commercial practice this adds weight to the definition of what your work is and what it is not. However you distribute it, print your website details on your book to promote your online portfolio.

Using the web **>** These extracurricular activities all share the same core factor: they are arenas for uncompromised, unadulterated, self-initiated work. And they all have the same benefits of allowing you to develop and change your work and reinvigorate your creative juices, as well as ultimately bringing more work, directly or indirectly.

Web-based activity is an extracurricular activity of its own and arguably a more oblique approach to promoting you and your work to the wider world.
As touched on earlier, there's a place both for traditional self-promotion and its associated forms of networking as well as the more serendipitous web-based approach exemplified by the YouTube phenomenon. A blog probably provides the potential for background 'build' to your reputation – that is, of course, if anyone of consequence to your work visits the site and reads what's on it.
It's worth reiterating that your interpersonal skills are important here. Don't be tempted to do or say something online that you wouldn't do or say face to face. However, web-based promotion is arguably no more of a gamble than mailing out a postcard that may well go straight in the bin. Ultimately, you need to devise your own strategy, and some of this can be motivated as much by what forms of promotion interest you as by what is the most solidly effective method.

Courtesy and empathy **>** When planning your promotional strategy, think about how busy your target art directors might be, with deadlines looming and colleagues breathing down their necks. One of the most fundamental things that can be overlooked, if you become too blinkered by focusing on promoting yourself, is that this is not just about you and what you want. People are busy and you are just one of hundreds, if not thousands, of illustrators who might contact them and want their attention. For this reason it's essential to empathize with your intended audience and try to anticipate how your approach might be received. Failure to think in this way is the equivalent of a poor telephone manner. Remember your interpersonal skills when approaching someone, be it directly, person to person, or via any form of promotion. Make it as easy and enjoyable as possible for designers and art directors to see what you do. If you do this well, the contact should be memorable, and that's important for obvious reasons. Despite the immediacy of e-mail and the web, courtesy and consideration still go a long way. A bad first impression in a professional context is hard to shift.

Marion Deuchars

Can you provide a brief outline of your studies?

> BA in Illustration and Printmaking, Duncan of Jordanstone College of Art, Dundee, Scotland; MA, Illustration, Royal College of Art, London.

How well did your studies prepare you for working as an illustrator?

> They did well in preparing me to think uniquely and to be the best artist I could be. That, in the long term, was probably more useful than teaching me how to resolve an illustration brief. It was not good with regard to running a business, which essentially you have to do once you leave college. However, commissioned work started slowly (it was a recession) and that gave me time to work out how to prepare invoices, advertise etc.

What were your first experiences of working as an illustrator?

> I spent quite a lot of time compiling names and addresses of art directors from magazines, publishers and advertising companies. This was my main target source for work. I called them, sent them examples of my work, tried to make appointments to show my portfolio. I would go to bookshops, newsagents, look through design books, sourcing work I liked and seeing who was responsible for it. I saw art directors from many different companies. It was useful feedback and most were encouraging. It was enough to keep me producing work, and through these contacts, work did start to trickle in.

Any memorable incidents from this period?

> I remember finding my first commissions quite hard. It was hard enough to please the art director, but they then had to please their client. I also used to take rejections quite personally. I think when I first started out, I worried too much about each job rather than trying to enjoy the work a bit more.

How did you cope financially?

> It took about five years before I was financially stable. The biggest expense then was art materials and publicity. I used to teach in Ipswich two days a week for two years and then moved to teaching one day a week in various London colleges. That paid my studio rent.

Are you methodical in your working life?

> Yes, I would say I'm pretty disciplined and conscientious. I nearly always produce work on time and most of the time fulfil the brief. It's not that difficult when your business only involves one person.

Do you work from home or a studio?

> I never worked from home. As soon as I left college about 10 of us set up a studio straight away.

What do you feel are the benefits?

> Working alone suits many people but I need social interaction, and I like 'going to work' rather than going to a room in my house. I felt early on that being in a studio made me feel more confident when I met clients. It felt more professional. Part of my creative process also involves a fair amount of tea making, chatting and generally avoiding sitting down to work straight away.

Do you have an agent/rep?

> Yes.

What do you like or dislike about it?

> I like that my agent takes care of all aspects of my work except for making it. It helps me to concentrate on what I do best. My agent also deals with all fee negotiation, another job I don't like. Many of the big, interesting jobs seem to come through my agent. It's harder for some of the advertising agencies to contact an individual illustrator. Many commissions are also quite complicated in terms of licence fees, client needs, changes etc. An agent is able to deal with these in a much more consistent and professional, and less emotional, way than I can.

What kind of promotional activity do you do?

> I now publish my own books, so that is my main promotional activity. I also have a website and work Facebook page. My agent also promotes my work.

Can you imagine working without an agent?

> I can imagine working without one, but for now, it works well for me. If I didn't have an agent, I'd be poorer.

Do you have a website?

> Yes. I think nowadays people expect to find a website or at least

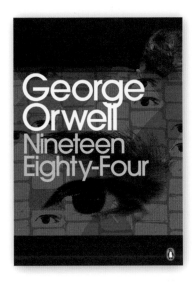
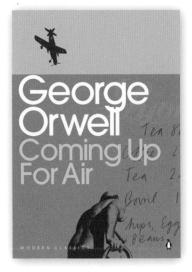
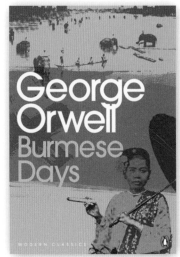

121

some way of sourcing information about you and your work.

How does having a website affect your relationship with your agent?

> It requires some honesty on my part, as clients can easily contact me and offer me jobs directly, which they do. In the main, unless they are existing clients or friends, I put all work through my agent.

What social media do you use regularly?

> Facebook, Twitter, Pinterest, Statigram. On a good day, it feels nice and important. It also works well as a kind of archive. On a bad day, I wonder why I delve into the 'other world'.

Is social media important in promoting your work? Do you see a return?

> At the moment, yes. I believe so, but it's hard to prove. Mind you, it was equally hard to see a return with my old promotion strategy; sending out printed matter with my work on it to hundreds of art directors. Paper, postage, print, effort, sometimes rewarded with

a few enquiries. But you have to promote, so promote in whatever means are relevant to the time.

Has the promotional landscape changed in the last six years?

> Massively. It's like two different worlds: before the computer and after the computer. I feel like a relic sometimes when I speak to students.

Do you see clients face to face?

> Very rarely, no time, no need, but quite nice when it happens.

Have you had any bad experiences with clients?

> In the 20 years I've been working, very few. The issues that have come up are normally about 'usage' or plagiarism. Disputes are quite rare. On the few occasions, my agent has sent a letter with some serious undertones and that has normally been enough.

How do you feel about dealing with contracts?

> I don't really like dealing with contracts, that's why I have an agent. When I have to sign a contract, I just remember to read it before signing!

Have you ever turned work down for reasons other than not being available?

> Yes, if I don't think I'm right for the job, it's too difficult, or I don't like the subject or client.

What do you like most about being an illustrator?

> Variety, being my own boss. Making art for a living is a privilege in life.

What do you like least?

> Having to make changes to artwork.

What do you think is the future of illustration?

> We will always need and be interested in pictures and image makers. The picture can be more immediate than the word, so I think the future is rosy.

Offer one piece of advice to a new illustrator.

> Try to be unique.

Marion Deuchars

Let's make some GREAT FINGERPRINT ART

Opposite: Marion's book *Let's Make Some Great Fingerprint Art* (Laurence King Publishing)
Above left: *A Family Affair* for *The Guardian*
Above right: *Guantanamo Camp* for *The Guardian*
Right: *Orwell in Spain* for Penguin Books

Chapter 7
Studios

Your studio > When you start your career, it's likely you will find yourself working from home. When you first leave college this will probably be your only option financially, and in many ways it's a very practical way to begin and keeps costs to a minimum.

Working from home feels like a luxury for a while. No travelling, no institutional work environment, but rather all your favourite things and home comforts around you: music, coffee, TV breaks if you feel like it. I remember enjoying it immensely, until I began finding myself popping out to buy a fifth pint of milk and another packet of biscuits (to add to the four pints already bought that day), simply in order to have a conversation or some personal interaction with another human being.

Illustration is a rather solitary activity and, depending on your temperament, it can become debilitatingly lonely. Some people are perfectly happy working from home and get their dose of social interaction by going out in the evenings. Others will feel isolated very quickly. The alternative is to take the plunge financially and work from a studio, either shared or on your own.

Initially, financial considerations will have much to do with your decision, but beyond the question of affordability is what suits you, your temperament and your work best. Some swear by working from home; others work from studios and would be horrified at the idea of having to work from home, even with a room set aside as a studio.

I have friends in both camps. Most share studios, but a couple at least are totally immovable when it comes to the idea of taking a studio space. They claim they can't imagine being able to concentrate enough to work with other people around. You will, with a bit of time, find which is best for you. There are pros and cons to both choices; ultimately, it's a matter of personal preference.

Jonny Hannah's shed

Working from home: the pros > The time saved and hassle avoided in not having to travel has to be one of the greatest benefits of being based at home. Combine this with being able to create your own personalized work environment, where you can surround yourself with the things that inspire you, and you have a working life that many people would envy and kill for.

If you live in a rented flat or house, you can probably claim some portion of your rent and utility bills as business expenses, further adding to the financial savings. If work dries up for a while, you don't have the added burden of a second rent to pay. By minimizing your overheads you minimize your risks, which is important for someone trying to get a new business off the ground.

Scott Garrett's
spare-room studio

If you have a lot of work on, or a short overnight deadline to deal with, you can work all night and fall into bed at whatever hour you want, without having to consider travelling.

Architectural illustrator Robbie Polley, who is based in London, works from home, and for him the flexible working hours are a big plus:

'I like the ease of getting to and from work. I can work in pyjamas if I like. I have very flexible working hours, which is important when I'm very busy – I might have to work all night or from early morning. If I start at 5am I can easily do a full day before lunch with no interruptions. Working from home was a financial consideration at first, although now it's a preference. I work much better alone. I don't like anyone seeing the way I work, as I'm quite self-conscious. I prefer to get on without any talk or without people looking over my shoulder. As pros go, I think those are pretty nice benefits and whoever has worked from home will likely remember those golden moments. The problem is that the novelty factor can wear thin.'

**Working from home:
the cons**

> Once the novelty of falling out of bed and going straight to your desk has worn off, there are a number of things that can diminish the appeal of working from home.

There's the question of discipline. Are you disciplined enough not to waste a huge amount of your time faffing about at home, rather than getting on with your work? As a freelancer, this question of self-control is always there, whether you work from home or in a studio. Of necessity, there is the helpful, externally

Jason Ford in his studio

applied, discipline of a looming deadline. However, much of what you need to get done, over and above physically producing artwork on time, is not subject to this helpful pressure. If you are prone to avoidance and distractions, working from home could prove to be your undoing.

London-based Andy Martin worked from various studios for many years before opting to be based at home. This was to facilitate a shift to working in film and moving image, and he needed development time without the added financial pressure of studio overheads. Having worked both in studios and at home, Martin sees both sides: 'I've had various studios over 20 years, ranging from leaking garrets in a pre-youth-logged East End to swanky carpeted affairs with portholes in the interior doors (very 1980s). I work better alone for sure, and I know that I'm a bad influence on those around me who are trying to concentrate – and am easily distracted myself.'

However, he's equally honest about the solitary nature of working from home: 'I've learned to spot the demon isolation early and I can be out of the studio and on the bus or train – destination anywhere – within minutes. It's either that or entrapping the men who come round to read the electricity meter, shouting through the letter box at passing strangers or talking to my radio.'

Loneliness affects people differently according to their temperament, but can take another form: professional isolation. You can talk to illustrator friends, but working alone means you have to learn the ropes of being an illustrator on your own. By opting to work from home, alone, you miss out on shared information on clients, feedback on pricing and so on. It's likely, therefore, to be more difficult to find new clients. Chats that you might have in a shared studio can be informative forums during which contacts are compared, and who is commissioning what and where gets discussed. And you miss out on opportunities to meet someone's clients. A lot can arise from such chance meetings. The general creative buzz of being in a studio is easily overlooked and hard to quantify in terms of cost, but if you experience it while in a studio set-up, you would certainly miss it if you went back to working in isolation. Even travelling to and from a studio and being in an urban centre provides a creative stimulus that helps feed your work and keeps your visual batteries topped up – the kind of tangential benefit that can easily be taken for granted until you're deprived of it.

Brett Ryder

Illustrator, London

Do you have a studio or do you work from home?

> I work from home and have done since college.

What influenced your choice of current set-up?

> During college I found I preferred to work from home, where there were fewer distractions. I seemed to spend too much of my time in the college canteen looking at the girls from ceramics, or any other subject for that matter, but the ceramic girls seemed to be the prettiest.

Do you have a room set aside as a studio?

> I do now. Each time I've moved to a new flat or house I have made a conscious effort to improve my working environment: I now have my own room full of my own junk. If any unidentified object happens to have found its way into my room it is quickly evicted. If you have a studio at home other people like to think of it as the junk room, not an Aladdin's cave of hidden treasure. So don't be surprised if one day you enter and find a pair of dirty wellies and an old tennis racket leaning against the wall next to your box of treasured beer mats.

What do you think are the benefits of working from home? What do you like most about it?

> The obvious benefits are no distractions. You can do what you want and choose your own radio station. There are no overheads as such, just tea, vodka, gin and so on. You can wear what you want and feel comfortable, even if you're having an ugly day. You will also probably have a larger space to work in. I have a room, and have no idea how much the rent for the same space would be.

What are the downsides?

> The downsides are the flipside to the benefits. The lack of distractions is valuable, but it would be nice to hang out with other people (at work, at least – I'm not that lonely), talk about art, discuss projects and so on. Even though travelling to work is seen as a drag, it can be quite stimulating. There are some very strange people out there, although I don't necessarily advise talking to them or even smiling at them – I wouldn't want to put you in any danger.

How does your partner feel about you working from home?

> In general, they like having someone to wash up or hang out the washing, and complain to if it hasn't been done. I think in general it's seen as a nice thing – I'm usually home when they get back from work. The downside is not having a huge amount of gossip to share. You haven't seen anyone, but you have to listen to them moan about the journey home or their day at work, and can't reciprocate.

Is the consideration primarily financial or one of personal preference?

> There are pros and cons to working from home, but I couldn't change even if I wanted to as I need solitude to work and think.

Do you work better alone, uninterrupted in a private environment? Do you ever feel isolated?

> I have moved to a beautiful house in the country, but I have found it too isolated, combined with working at home. I am a city person at heart, and expect there are further moves ahead.

What, if anything, do you do to counteract the solitary nature of working from home?

> I go out and don't come home for days. Only joking – but I do have big nights out to blast away the cobwebs. I ride my motorcycle, I go climbing and I bought a dog who goes everywhere with me (nearly). We live just outside London so I go in regularly to see friends and go book shopping.

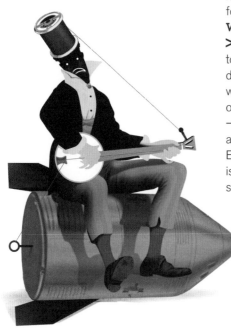

I've known many seemingly well-balanced people who, when working from home, get disproportionately upset and angry over work-related problems. When they've articulated what it was that bothered them, it was often nothing out of the ordinary. What changed their perception of it was feeling that it was unique to them. If they were alongside other illustrators on a daily basis, firstly, the working environment might dissipate some of the tension and, secondly, they might see at first hand other illustrators experiencing similar problems.

Luke Best, from the collective Peepshow, recognized the benefits of sharing with other illustrators very quickly:

'Most of us were at university together and it started as a website and a way of staying in touch and sharing contacts, and it's grown naturally from there. We were getting more and more group projects so it became necessary to have a space for us all to work in, rather than meeting in the pub. Also, working at home became very uninspiring and I thought being around other people in the same situation would push me to get more work. It's good to have people that you trust around you for advice and help on certain jobs. Because we are all friends, the studio is also a fun place to be.'

The ability to separate your work and home life can be important if you want to establish some degree of balance in your life. Being freelance means you usually have little control over the flow of work – it's often feast or famine, and the so-called feast can be overwhelming enough, even without living under the same roof as it. However much you love what you do, you are likely to want to switch off from illustration at times, and this can be very difficult when it's there calling to you from the spare room or the corner of your living room.

The pro of a proportion of your rent and utility bills being set against tax as a business expense can have a sting in its tail. If you happen to own your own home, you can certainly offset some of the costs, as discussed; but when you come to sell your house or flat any increase in value, which would ordinarily be free from capital gains tax, might become subject to it because of your use of your home for business. This point is complicated and best addressed by an accountant, but this potential sting should not be overlooked.

The studio option: the pros

> Deciding whether or not to take a studio solely in terms of what it will cost is very short-sighted. Many of the pros far outweigh any cost burdens, and in the long term you may well reap greater financial rewards.

If you have enjoyed a college environment, with other people working alongside you, the shift to working from home, alone all day, will come as a shock to the system. Sharing a studio can alleviate that shock, and help prevent any loneliness you might fall prey to working from home.

I think having a studio also puts you in a different frame of mind about your working life. Going to a place of work that is yours, for which you pay rent,

'I like to leave the house in the morning, pick up breakfast and walk five minutes to my studio. I prefer having a space where the only thing I can do is work and be creative. When I leave the studio and go home I can enjoy after-work time apart from the projects that surround me at the studio.'

Romy Blümel, Illustrator

working there all day and then going home reinforces the idea that you are, effectively, a small business and, as such, should be thinking like one. It also helps you make that necessary mental transition from amateur to professional, and can focus your thinking and help you become more disciplined.

New York-based Sam Weber prefers a studio working environment for a number of reasons:

'It was partially a space thing. My apartment is fairly small, and to work comfortably, with enough room to spread out and mess around, getting a workspace outside of the home seemed like a fairly sensible thing to do. Even as a student, I always liked working away from home. I really enjoy that separation of work and relaxation. There are days when I regret having to trudge home after a long day at work, and sometimes wish I could more casually pick away at projects when the mood strikes me. However, I enjoy the focus and routine that heading out of the house every day allows me. At this stage in my artistic life, being around other working artists is really helpful. I have the chance to watch other people work, ask them questions and get honest answers. My studio mates are all hardworking, and it's good motivation to watch them work and succeed, and make beautiful things.'

Creating artworks is a relatively small part of the work as a whole. You are a business. Every business has core concerns, and the fact that illustration is a creative activity doesn't mean you can ignore them. Cash flow, for example, is a business's lifeblood. If you ignore it, you'll find a huge amount of mental space is consumed by dealing with the ensuing problems. Getting into the right frame of mind is essential and having a place of work, outside your home, is key to this.

Lara Harwood's Chocolate Factory studio, where her computer is not the focal point

David Lucas

Children's book illustrator, London

From *The Skeleton Pirate* by David Lucas

Do you have a studio or do you work from home?

> I've had a studio for the last seven years, but worked from home previously.

What made you choose to work from a studio?

> My work wasn't going well. I was isolated, had problems planning, concentrating and focusing. I tended to go round in circles. In common with lots of creative people I am fairly obsessive and live in my own head too much. I need other people around to help me be balanced. It was deeply reassuring to find, once I'd moved into a shared studio, that my circumstances had been the problem – not me.

How far do you have to travel to your studio?

> My ten-minute cycle ride along the canal towpath is the perfect journey to work.

Do you find the studio expensive?

> It's expensive, but essential. It is a huge mistake for me ever to let money worries rule my decision-making. They are a factor, of course, but must not be allowed to dominate. In my experience it is vital to aim high, both artistically and in life. I generally find that if I raise my sights, events conspire in my favour – fate smiles on me. If I am too cautious things begin to unravel.

Does the expense of a studio ever cause you concern?

> Yes, but mostly when I am in a negative state of mind more generally. I have marked peaks and troughs in my creative work, and am usually in a low just after a major project. All kinds of things seem threatening, including my overdraft. After taking a break, centring myself and approaching things more bravely, I have always found that things work out.

Do you share the studio?

> Yes, there are six others, and another 15 or so in adjoining rooms. I can only imagine wanting a studio to myself if I was much older or so fantastically successful that I wanted to hide away from the world.

Do you prefer a multidisciplinary studio?

> I am the only one in my studio working in children's books, and I suppose I would prefer it if there were a few people working in the same area as me.

What do you like about it?

> Above all, it's fun, but it's good to be able to ask casually for feedback or advice or technical help without it being any special effort. Even a tiny thing like being able to borrow things makes a big difference. Working alongside others every day also gives me a clearer picture of who I am – what I am good or bad at – which is invaluable when a huge part of my job is being as much myself as possible. I can get a better sense of my strengths and weaknesses. I think self-knowledge is vital if you're selling the products of your own imagination. Sharing space has made me better at valuing the differences between myself and others, better at appreciating others' strengths – admiring them rather than being jealous or threatened. But, at the same time, seeing someone effortlessly achieve something I myself struggle with is also a challenge, making me less lazy about my failings. To me it is so obviously beneficial: I stand far more chance of making the most of my talents if I work alongside successful, talented people. Sharing a studio also broadens my horizons in an effortless, almost accidental way, and I find out about music, books and websites I otherwise wouldn't. I have a strong tendency to narrow my horizons and focus on what is most me, which is an important part of my work. But left unchecked, that leads to my world shrinking alarmingly. I become scared of novelty, and my creativity begins to wither and die. Being around others is like oxygen.

If you could change one thing about your work set-up, what would it be?

> I'd like there to be a few more girls around – the kind who would flatter me and tell me how wonderful I am and laugh at even my feeblest jokes.

On the practical side, shared studios mean shared bills. Sharing phone and fax lines and a broadband service can help keep costs down. The same applies to general utilities. However, while these may be important considerations when starting out, they are the minor benefits of sharing a studio.

Working with your peers or, even better, within a studio of illustrators who have been working for a few more years than you can give you invaluable access to other people's experience.

I worked in various studios and not always with other illustrators. Prior to joining the Big Orange, a studio of nine other illustrators, I worked in one nearer to where I lived, alongside four girls doing wholly unrelated work. One did fashion prediction, one knitwear, another lingerie and the fourth bespoke rubber wear for her fetishist clientele. I was the sole illustrator among them. It was fun on a daily basis, but the real benefits of sharing a studio struck me when I moved to the Big Orange.

My experience at Big Orange was frankly an epiphany. There were ten illustrators working alongside one another, but no one competing directly with anyone else for work because stylistically everyone was different – but very good at what they did. Accordingly, there was a confidence in the air. Nobody felt they needed to prove anything, and no one was worried about anyone else taking work off them, so we shared a lot of experience and information. We would discuss fees, quotes we needed to put in for design or advertising jobs, how to deal with tricky problems with clients and how to play such conversations with them, or even make recommendations of who to show work to.

'The studio makes my life more comfortable; it's better for my head and so much better for working. I also use the eyes of the others in the studio. Even if they don't look at the work, they participate in it without knowing. This enriches everything.'

Marc Boutavant,
Illustrator

On a more casual level, someone might walk past my desk on their way to make a cup of tea when I was struggling with a composition that didn't work. 'That yellow in the top there is throwing it all out' might be mentioned in passing – and that would crack the deadlock. The studio did a lot of work at that time for the *New Law Journal*, and the jobs involved arcane points of law that had to be expressed simply in visual terms. Roughs would be shown around, opinions expressed and ridicule poured on lame ideas, but always in a spirit of goodwill. I'm certain I learned more in that studio than I ever did at college.

Sharing a studio also addresses the question of going stir-crazy when working at home. Given how important interpersonal skills are to an illustrator, remembering how to speak and hold a conversation is another of the benefits you can derive from a shared studio environment.

Going home is a great part of going out to work. London-based Jimmy Turrell, on being asked what he liked most about working from a studio, responded: 'The division between work and play. I love the feeling of being totally relaxed when I come home from the studio.'

As an illustrator, you need to be able to juggle all the various aspects of your professional activity and your own life. Tempting though it is to see them as one and the same thing, they should be kept separate for the sake of your sanity. Leaving work and switching off is an essential discipline. A tutor once told me that it was important to think about things other than just art and illustration. 'Otherwise,' he said, 'you'll be like a surgeon who comes home and spends all evening talking about the operations he's performed that day. It can be very boring for other people.'

The studio option: the cons

> The arguments for taking a studio rather than working from home are not just about the danger of your personal hygiene habits slipping. It is good to place parameters on your working life and establish rhythms and routines of work as soon as possible. This may seem anathema to the new illustrator who loves living and breathing the activity, who relishes being able to work through until dawn or roll out of bed in the middle of the night when inspiration strikes. If you are disciplined you can make it work for you, and it's certainly easier if you can have a dedicated space or room at home to call a studio.

Having a studio can be a significant expense to bear, not only because of the rent, but also because of the electricity and phone bills. Such costs are there even when the work isn't. They can be a major concern, but studio set-ups can introduce other significant considerations, depending on whether you're joining an established studio or setting one up yourself, with or without the help of others.

Roderick Mills's studio

Predictably enough, larger metropolitan areas tend to have higher rental costs. If you are organizing a studio, you may be the person who signs the lease and is therefore ultimately responsible for paying the rent regardless of whether the studio is full or half empty. For such reasons, there are often several signatories to any lease, so there is shared responsibility and a shared pressure to get any desk spaces filled as soon as they become vacant. If you are involved in a set-up where you have more space than you need individually, then you risk having to make up any shortfalls in rent. The same applies to shared utility costs. If they are divided eight ways as opposed to four, it's a lot less expensive for all concerned. Furthermore, a rental lease will be for a fixed period, and once you sign you are generally stuck with it and the attendant responsibilities. Some leases allow for subletting, so if you choose to leave before your lease is up you can sublet to a third party. However, you are still ultimately responsible if your 'tenant' fails to pay the rent.

Getting on with your studio buddies is important, both socially and for your working habits. Some people like to work in near silence, others like a lot of activity or loud music. Even the choice of music can be a friction point if it upsets someone's ability to work. Also, if you are all jointly responsible for the studio, you need to be able to get on with and trust one another, so that if things get stressful with the rent and bills, you can work together to resolve the problems.

There are various studio set-ups and not all require such onerous commitments from someone who is just starting out as an illustrator, but all have costs attached. Some people only feel comfortable taking on a studio once their career has some momentum behind it, and a fairly steady flow of work has started coming in.

If you're working long hours or are forced into doing a very late night – if not a full 'overnighter' – having to get home afterwards can be a pain. High urban rents can mean you have to locate your studio in an area that's less central than you would like. Lower rents are often found in areas where transport links are less than ideal, and this can impact on your late-night journey home or on your travelling times generally.

The greater part of the discussion about whether or not to work from a studio really has to focus on the pros – the tangible and not so tangible benefits of a place of work that is separate from your home.

Romy Blümel

Can you provide a brief outline of your studies?

> I graduated with a degree in Illustration from the University of Applied Sciences in Hamburg.

How well did your studies prepare you for working as an illustrator?

> I did not learn much about how to get commissions or work with clients and towards a deadline. None of my tutors had much experience in editorial illustration or advertising. What gave me an insight into working for commercial clients was an internship at a graphic design studio in Berlin during my final year. There, I learned how to use illustration in a functional context and how to execute a commission. We made posters for bands, catalogues for fairs, websites, brochures etc. with an illustrative approach.

What were your first experiences of working as an illustrator?

> I took part in an illustration competition and was exhibited in Paris. I started working with two independent theatre groups designing posters, drew a storyboard for a short film and designed a record and a website for a Berlin-based band. All of these projects where instructive, but none was paid. With a website as my portfolio, including these projects, I started to contact art directors. Often, I received positive reactions but obtained only two editorial commissions in six months. I found an agency in Berlin and

I soon received enquiries from magazines, advertising agencies and newspapers.

Any memorable incidents from this period?

> I remember the first editorial commission I received. A friend of mine was asked to do it, but didn't have time. She recommended me. Somehow I believed I had to work in a similar style to her. She does collages; my portfolio was filled with paintings. So, I did a collage. The client printed it but didn't hire me again. I can't remember why I thought a popular magazine would hire me to copy someone else's style. After that I tried to complete my portfolio with a range of features. But when I got hired, clients always referred to the work I did for private projects. I learned that clients look for uniqueness.

How did you cope financially?

> In the first year I worked at a bar two or three nights a week, at a restaurant on the weekends and got some financial support from my family, as well.

Are you methodical in your working life?

> I work Monday to Friday from 10am to 8pm, often Saturdays. When working on a commission I read the brief, then find out everything I need to fulfil the task, like measurements, deadline, layout, and then I do something completely different for as long as I can to let the information settle. I have no method during the sketching phase. Sometimes, I do several detailed drawings, sometimes only one loose sketch.

Do you work from home or a studio?

> Six months after graduating I rented a spot in a studio with 11 other illustrators and designers. It was a great opportunity to meet experienced illustrators. They helped me start my business. Last year, I moved to a studio closer to home, shared with eight other artists.

What do you feel are the benefits?

> In both studios I have worked in so far I met other artists, who I collaborated with, and made friends of course, who I wouldn't have met working at home.

Do you have an agent/rep?

> I am represented in Germany, Switzerland and Austria by 2agenten in Berlin, and in the rest of the world by Heart Agency in London and New York.

What do you like or dislike about it?

> I don't have to canvass for clients and I am able to concentrate on my artistic work. To stay in touch with clients, make contracts and negotiate fees takes a lot of time. Both agencies I work with have a big client base, and this is an advantage that I wouldn't have had in such a short time working on my own. Also, I know these people like the work I do, believe in me and therefore support me.

What kind of promotional activity do you do?

> Almost nothing myself. I have a Facebook page where I post links or announce exhibitions etc. Very

Fashion Retail for the *Sunday Telegraph* magazine

Left: *The King in the Brothel* for *Hinz&Kunzt* magazine
Below: *Girl* (personal work)
Bottom: *A Tale of Two Tea Parties* for *Condé Nast Traveller* magazine

few of my clients follow these activities, and I'm not sure if it has any useful promotional purpose. I also have an online portfolio on the websites of both agencies.

Can you imagine working without an agent?

> I've barely worked alone since I graduated. I have never had a bad experience working with agents. If I didn't have an agent I would have concentrated on personal projects, probably with another job on the side. I'm impressed by illustrators who are able to promote themselves enough to make a living and at the same time advance artistically.

Do you have a website?

> Yes. I kept a portfolio of recent illustrations on it. I often changed the layout and updated the work. Recently I decided to delete the portfolio, because most of my work can also be seen on the websites of my agencies. At the moment I'm rethinking my personal website. One idea is using it only for personal work as an addition to the portfolios already existing online.

How does having a website affect your relationship with your agent?

> I keep it as an extension to the promotion that my agents do for me. If I get enquiries from clients based on my website, then I connect them with my agent.

What social media do you use regularly?

> Facebook. My friends can follow my work. People who are not linked to my website or the agencies I work with can see it.

Is social media important in promoting your work? Do you see a return?

> I don't think that the way I use Facebook has any promotional function. Probably, I could get more 'fans' by doing regular posts, and the possibility of making a professional contact might rise. I have never got in touch with a client through Facebook. The chance that a possible client will look at my whole portfolio after reading a post is very low.

Do you see clients face to face?

> Maybe once a year. Most of my clients work outside Berlin and the commissions I receive are often urgent. I only meet clients for briefings, never to promote myself. But I believe getting in touch with people face to face increases your chance of being remembered.

Have you had any bad experiences with clients?

> Twice in the past four years I executed a commission as agreed, but unfortunately the client was unhappy with the outcome. The first time the client opted for a photograph instead, which was frustrating. The second time I worked with a client who wasn't willing to make amendments and didn't want to pay a cancellation fee. Luckily my agent could come to a compromise both times.

Have you ever turned work down for reasons other than not being available?

> Last year I illustrated a regular column in a German magazine.

I was very happy to have the opportunity. After a few weeks, I realized that it was creating stress. The deadline usually collided with other deadlines. The art director asked me to develop more sketches each time. I was increasingly unsatisfied, but the client became more and more keen on them. It felt like a misunderstanding and after three months I cancelled the column.

What do you like most about being an illustrator?

> The random input I get with each commission.

What do you like least?

> Making compromises.

What do you think is the future of illustration?

> More and more illustrators who work digitally are entering the business. They are able to execute commissions quickly and amendments are easier. Clients will become used to commissioning illustrators in a shorter time. Another change caused by globalization is an increasing mix of styles and cultural influences. It might be difficult to hire unique and exceptional artists in the future.

Offer one piece of advice to a new illustrator.

> Develop a portfolio that shows your interest in the visual world, without worrying about creating images that are marketable.

Chapter 8
Agents

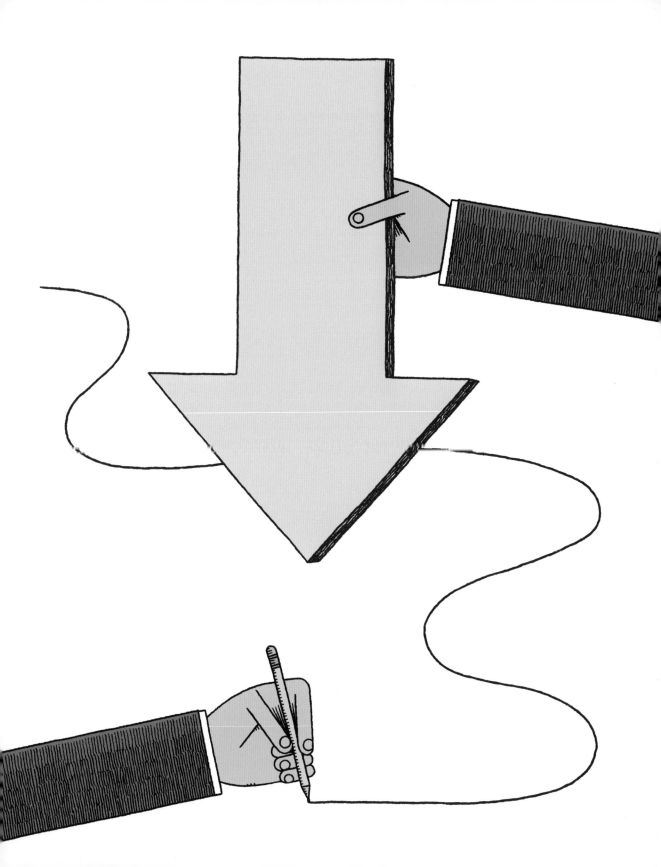

Why do you want an agent? > Many illustrators, especially those just starting out, view acquiring the services of an agent, or getting themselves represented, as a key objective as soon as they leave college, without considering what this means.

I suspect that the reason is insecurity. A college environment provides a framework of meaning and purpose, as well as a support network for student illustrators. Many will be daunted by the idea that once school is out they are on their own. Illustration is a freelance, self-employed career choice, and while most may pay lip service to accepting this, many will be apprehensive about the reality of it.

Leaving college is a big step, but stepping out with the understanding that you are immediately a 'sole trader', a small business that needs to bring in work or starve, is a daunting prospect. Choosing a career that involves seeking full-time employment may have its own difficulties, but it doesn't require quite as much self-motivation. For many, I think the agent is seen as a de facto employer, creating an illusion of security and employment by being a source of immediate and constant commissions. In fact, it simply doesn't work like that. The sooner you accept that you are effectively on your own and that your ability to succeed or fail in supporting yourself is down to you alone, the sooner you will be able to adapt to the lifestyle involved.

It is important to understand what agents do for their represented illustrators and what the pros and cons of having one are, so that you can make an informed choice about whether you want or need one. There are also the differences between agencies to consider, which should influence your choice if you decide you want an agent.

What does an agent do? > In its most basic form, the role of the agent is to bring the work of an artist to the attention of potential clients who may wish to use that particular artist's style of work.

Agents do this in a number of different ways, but their role amounts to strategic promotion of the artist and his or her work. This is done via printed promotional material – bespoke items created by the agency, pages taken in an assortment of annuals, web pages and so on. An agent can harness the reputation of the whole to promote the individual: a new artist appearing alongside well-respected and established illustrators will benefit by association. Alternatively, an agency might produce cards for individual artists and mail them to its client list, or use them at meetings to draw the client's attention to a new artist.

Promotion also comes about because of the general attention that will be paid to a particular agency's roster, based on its reputation either for specializing in a certain kind of work or for representing interesting work. Since the role of an agent is to seek commissions for their roster of artists, the agency should have a considerable pool of clients, which forms a marketplace to which they can take your work.

Whether or not agents go to regular meetings to see potential clients with portfolios of work is determined partly by the agency's staffing and workload, but also by how open clients are to having meetings to look through portfolios on a speculative basis. I would say that websites have reduced the demand for face-to-face meetings and speculative viewings of one or several portfolios. That said, if an agent has a fairly well-established working relationship with a client, but they have never actually met, both parties might be prepared to meet and use the opportunity to look through some work. I've found that in setting up such meetings, the client may be interested in seeing some specific portfolios, 'favourites' they may have spotted on the website but haven't yet had the opportunity to use. In those instances, I'll take along the requested books but also those of others I think they might like, be they new artists or ones who have been with the agency a while.

If I am going to see a new client, I'll probably take along a 'group book' as well as two or three individual portfolios. In the meeting itself, I'll note who he or she particularly likes when they are going through the group book and then offer to courier over the individual portfolios for them to look at in their own time.

Meetings with clients also take place if they want to discuss a particular project. If it relates to a specific artist, they might ask that he or she be present as well. Alternatively, clients may wish to give the agent a broad overview of what they are working on, with a view to finding out which artists might be suitable for their purposes. This also provides an opportunity for an agent to bring specific artists to a client's attention.

Jason Ford visits his
agent's office

Whether or not the clients actually meet the artists is partly down to circumstances and partly down to how protective an agent is. One agency in the UK used to be renowned for never letting artists speak to or meet clients. Absolutely everything was conducted via the agent, from submission of roughs, to giving feedback on work, to actual delivery. It does not seem a practical or particularly satisfying way of operating – I suspect the majority of agents feel the same, and doubt that many operate in this way. Most will work on the basis that once the fees and the contract have been worked out, it's best to let the artist and client talk directly. This reduces the chances of mistakes because of poorly conveyed information, and allows the working relationship to develop in an unfettered manner. The agent is there should either party have a problem with how the job is proceeding. This might be radio silence from the artist, or a change in the brief, or mission creep on the part of the client.

Once a job is up and running, an artist might meet a client for a face-to-face briefing or delivery and discussion of roughs. It depends on where both parties are based, how necessary the client feels a meeting is and how quickly work is needed. Sometimes an artist works repeatedly for the same client, communicating via the phone or e-mail, and neither party ever feels the need to meet.

Wladimir Marnich

Marnich Design

What was your first experience of working with an illustrator?
> Commissioning illustrations for *Tentaciones* – we had several illustrators who collaborated regularly on the different sections of the supplement. It was a good experience – the style and 'tone of voice' were clearly defined and therefore easy to understand, not only for me, but for the illustrators.

When do you use illustration?
> Whenever I can. As long as it fits with the project I am working on, which is nearly all the time.

Where do you find talent?
> I keep an eye on things that I see and like. Then I try to find out who these people are, often through the

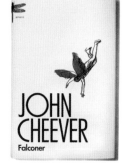
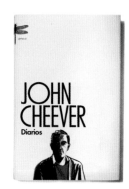

internet or making a few phone calls.

What do you feel are illustration's strengths?
> The great variety of styles and its flexibility. Unlike photography you don't need a group of people, and changes can be easily made.

Have you found illustrators open to art direction?
> Usually I find we have a good relationship. I try not to interfere too much, and look for people I relate to personally and professionally.

How do you find working with them as creative individuals?
> They see things in a different way. I like being surprised by their approach to a brief.

Do you ever have to reject artwork? On what grounds?
> Rather than rejecting work, we try to change direction or find alternatives. The few times that I rejected work it was because I noticed a lack of interest or effort from the illustrator. It is easy to see when they are not interested in what they are doing.

What kind of promotional items work best for you?
> Something simple. I just want to see the work, not how fancy or clever a promo is. No long Flash animations, tricky-to-open boxes or puzzles to put together!

Do you see many illustrators with their portfolios?
> Unfortunately not many come to see me. They send e-mails with website details – a pity. I enjoy the meetings, provided they don't go on forever. I like direct contact, even if it's only on the phone; I like knowing who I'm working with and what they are like.

What do you look for in a portfolio?
> I just want to see what kind of work they can do. I like to know if they have one style or several. I look at use of space, colour, shape, attention to detail and so on.

What is your experience of illustrators' websites?
> Usually they are a good source of information and inspiration. They work when they reflect the illustrator's work in a simple way. If a site is too slow I get bored and move on to someone else's.

How do you feel about working via an agent?
> No problem as long as they understand what I need in terms of work and budget, and don't interfere in my relationship with the illustrator.

How do you feel about contracts taking copyright?
> It's sneaky, although sometimes clients don't understand why they have to pay again to use an image in a different place or format.

What prevents you recommissioning someone?
> A lack of effort put into work, or a lack of understanding between us.

What do you feel about the future of illustration?
> I think technology will open up new ways of working, or even show us things we don't know exist. However, I don't think it will make pen and paper disappear. At least that's what I hope.

What would be your advice to a new, would-be illustrator?
> Do it because you love it, try to evolve and don't be a snob.

Once a potential client has turned into an actual client, it falls to the agent to negotiate a fee (and what usage rights are included in it) and to bill for the work once the job has been completed. The agreed fee is divided between the artist and the agent, with the agent's percentage being anything from 25 to 40 per cent (an average, I believe, is around 33 per cent). Once the agency is paid, it pays the artist his or her percentage of the agreed fee.

How all this works in practice varies a great deal, as each agency has a different culture, greatly dictated by its principles. The pros and cons of having an agent are fairly generally applicable, but certain agencies may well ameliorate many of the perceived downsides of having an agent because of their particular culture, while others, through their particular way of working, may diminish the usual pros. There are all sorts out there.

The advantages of having an agent

> The first notable benefit of having an agent is access to someone else's professional experience and advice. You may well have friends who are illustrators and can therefore turn to them for advice or to air concerns, but hopefully your agent will be there in a professional capacity to advise you, and be a sounding board for thoughts and worries you might have as you find your feet. He or she can also provide an objective opinion on you and your work and perhaps guide you on how to develop your growing profile, knowing which jobs are worth doing and which ones are sometimes worth giving a miss.

While some illustrators are perfectly content to operate without an agent and are able to handle some larger, more complicated commissions, an agent will have much more experience of negotiation and client liaison, simply because they do it all the time. A lone illustrator might take on three larger, complicated commissions in a year, whereas an agent is likely to handle maybe three in a week, which amounts to a lot of learning and experience. That should not be underestimated. I would say a great deal of negotiating is instinctive, and someone's instincts for such matters are honed by immersion in the activity.

'A really good agent facilitates the process in every way. They know their artist, and how they will react in different situations, which can often help if the job is pressured in any way.'

Sarah Thomson, Art Buyer

Having an agent also means that you have the support of a team of people behind you, who will help raise your profile and bring you more commissions. Furthermore, while you work they have a vital interest in getting invoices paid, so they chase up payment due for work that you've done, lifting this kind of administrative burden from you and hopefully improving your cash flow.

An agent can reach a greater audience through an established and well-managed database and promotional activity, be it via the web or good old-fashioned print. Since it is an agency's business to bring its artists' work to the attention of as many clients as possible, the agent will be continually looking to expand his or her pool of potential clients. The agent's role is to establish good working relationships with commissioners of illustration and to look for new markets for their artists' work. This means that you have a dedicated organization looking for clients and contacts for you, which leaves you free to concentrate on the business of creating images.

In addition, an agency that takes pages in an annual may get preferential page rates because of the number of pages it is purchasing, and this discount is generally passed along to individual artists. Alternatively, the agency may pay part of the cost itself, effectively offering its artists a reduction on the page rate and hoping to defray some of the cost by negotiating a discount. Generally, an artist going into an annual via an agent will end up paying less for his or her page(s).

Strength in numbers > An agency's reputation can be a huge benefit to its artists, the whole being greater than the sum of its parts. A good roster of artists will keep clients interested in its activity, which means regular scouring of its website and looking through its promotional material. As a result you get attention, courtesy of the company you keep on your chosen agency's roster.

The strength of an agency, in terms of its artists and its reputation, is also very useful when resolving disputes with the occasional intransigent client. Because of the time and expense involved, it's not always worth considering legal action over relatively small sums of money. However, the potential for having the services of an entire roster of desirable artists revoked can often tip the balance in getting disputes settled equably.

This is the benefit of strength in numbers, and a lone illustrator trying to resolve a dispute with a client is unlikely to walk away with a fair resolution. He or she is likely to be faced with a take it or leave it decision. Thankfully, these situations don't arise too often, but when they do they can leave a lone artist feeling bruised and vulnerable.

Negotiating fees > Fee negotiations are often better handled by a third party. Not always, as I know some individual illustrators who are wily and tough negotiators – but they are the exception. If you are trying to establish a good working relationship with an art director, for example, you could find yourself accepting a fee that is much lower than it should be in order not to upset or annoy him or her. It's also not uncommon for some artists to feel uncomfortable about haggling over money. Some art directors will plead, nag and generally pressure you into accepting a job, insisting that their hands are tied on budget and that it would really help them out if you did the job for the fee they are offering. An agent can cajole, argue and generally insist on appropriate payment, without getting embarrassed or worried about upsetting the relationship with the art director and from a position of knowledge and experience.

I haven't yet come across an artist who has achieved better fees than an agent, but there are plenty of situations where the agent has secured higher fees through negotiation. This is particularly pertinent when dealing with larger commissions for design and advertising clients. Once fee levels climb beyond the top end of editorial levels, many artists can't imagine them going much higher and, consequently, don't know what to charge. If someone is accustomed to being paid £400 or $800 for an editorial illustration, but should be asking for ten times that sum for the same amount of work, the likelihood is that he or she will feel uncomfortable about doing so. An agent knows the value of the work and the rights being sold, and will confidently ask for that high fee and can argue if the client wants to negotiate. Given that this affects both your potential earning as well as the rights in your images, it's worth getting the professional advice an agent can provide.

Reviewing and negotiating contracts

> More and more, contracts are becoming the norm, even for small editorial jobs, and if you overlook the finer points you can find that you've signed away all rights in your image, beyond the first use you thought you were providing the illustration for. Furthermore, you could find that all future work for that particular client is governed by the first contract you signed. Sign in haste, repent at leisure. An agent is (or should be) more focused on reviewing and disputing contracts where necessary than a busy lone illustrator might be. A concern for me when I review contracts is that if something is agreed once, for one artist who may be less bothered (or more careless) about signing away rights, this effectively sets precedents that can be difficult to go back on for another artist. I have also found that the roster of artists that an agency represents provides leverage in negotiating contracts. If a client is dealing with a lone illustrator, they might say sign or we'll use someone else. In dealing with an agency that has a dozen or more artists the commissioner might wish to use at some point, he or she is more likely to be flexible and concede certain points to get a workable contract that's acceptable to both parties, so that they know they can use any of the other artists on the agency's roster if they need to.

Signing a contract on an artist's behalf can sometimes be a contentious matter. Most clients do not worry overly, provided it is signed, but some want to ensure that either the artist signs the contract (which is not always practical) or that they see proof that the agent has the authority to sign contracts on the artist's behalf. To this end, you may be asked by an agent to sign paperwork that confirms that you grant your agent the right to sign and enter into contracts on your behalf. This is called a power of attorney and can be limited to cover only work undertaken via the agency, and any other stipulations that might be deemed necessary. If in doubt about such paperwork, have it checked so that you fully understand what you are agreeing to.

Advertising fees and licences

> The whole question of contracts and rights becomes a good deal more complicated, with more money at stake, when negotiating advertising fees and licences. The comparatively large sums of money that are offered for advertising work can be very tempting, and the unwary can sign away very valuable rights for a fraction of their worth. An agent's role is invaluable here. Advertising clients can be difficult to negotiate with and can place an artist under enormous pressure to agree to something, because they are generally in an incredible hurry. An agent's established relationship with advertising clients can help in these negotiations; knowing when to say no is as important as knowing when to say yes.

We were once approached by a client to produce some images for Nike, for point of sale and window displays. The initial offer, after we quoted £40,000 ($60,000), came back at £15,000 ($22,500), take it or leave it. The artist and I really needed the money, but thankfully the artist was experienced enough to understand that the fee was too low. I had to say no on the basis of acting in his best interest, even though it was a particularly tough time for both of us. The artist, however, could have chosen to accept the job over and above my advice, and if he had done so I would have had to put the best possible face on it and accept his decision, as ultimately I was representing and acting for him. He agonized but turned down the job, and the client walked away. For two days the artist and I had long, painful discussions about the sense of turning down that kind of commision, but we managed to convince ourselves that we had done the right thing. Three days after the client walked away, they came back with a reduced number of images and a fee that had risen to £25,000 ($37,500). Once the job started, various amendments took the fee up to £30,000 ($45,000), which was far more appropriate than the original £15,000 ($22,500) on the table. I have no doubt that the artist would have capitulated without the experience, advice and support of an agent.

The potential problems

> The most obvious negative in having an agent is the cost of the commission fees that an artist pays. While we are supposed to be looking at cons, I can't resist explaining that this can be a rather limited viewpoint. Agreed, you will pay between 25 and 40 per cent, depending on the kind of job and the rate of commission a particular agent charges. As a broad-stroke example, you will probably pay £300 ($450) commission on a job that pays £1000 ($1500), but you may not have got the work at all without the agent's involvement, or, if you had, you may well not have secured a fee of even £700 ($1050). In the end, the agent is providing services that you have to pay for. In many instances you won't see the tangible benefits of such services on every job, but when you do, you're likely to consider it money well spent.

However, you are in the position of having a middleman, someone who represents 'you' and your way of doing things to a third party in a way that you cannot really control. You can choose an agent because you think he or she is likely to represent you and your interests as faithfully as possible. Ultimately, it's a matter of trusting them – not only in how they deal with clients on a one-to-one basis, but also in how they show your work, and which examples they favour when doing so.

I remember as an illustrator turning up to a meeting with a client of my own and finding my then agent's assistant giving a presentation. It was done very badly and I was embarrassed to have witnessed it. It did lead me to question seriously how I was being represented to clients; your choice of agent is your choice of personal ambassador, so you want to get your representation right.

When you join an agency, you are judged by the company you keep as well as on your own merits. This is not for everyone. There are, however, pros and cons. If you really like the work of the other artists represented, you may benefit

Agency promotional cards

from it, as your work is benchmarked along the same lines as theirs. If you are among people whose work you don't like or feel doesn't complement your own, you may or may not stand out from the crowd within that particular agency. If you opt to be represented by an agent, you are one of a group. Depending on your choice of agent, you could be lost among a hundred other artists.

If you choose the wrong agent, you could end up represented by an agency that is not particularly associated with your kind of work. When potential clients are looking for a specific style of work, there may be certain agencies that are well known for handling that type of illustration, so if you're not in the right place, you may get overlooked. You wouldn't buy textiles at a timber merchant, would you?

Contractually, you may be tied to your agency for a set period of time. In some cases you may be expected to work exclusively via that agent, irrespective of any clients you may have established earlier in your career. You may also not be able to act totally independently any more. This depends on many factors, from agency culture to the form any given contract may take.

If you go straight to an agent from college, you may bypass the chance to start learning from your own experience, and the opportunity to establish your own client base and ways of doing things. Meeting clients face to face helps you develop your working relationship with art directors and designers. You may well make some mistakes, but being forced to sort out your own problems on a job boosts your confidence and will help you to be assertive about your work and how you are treated by clients. Assertive does not mean confrontational or having an attitude; it means not being too timid to speak your mind politely and firmly if you disagree with some aspect of how a job is going or how you are being treated. Some artists hate dealing with problems; they hate complaining and dread the idea of offending a client by speaking out and disagreeing with them. Doing things you don't enjoy is an important part of anyone's development, but learning to do so as a freelancer is particularly important. You're a small business and you need to know how to handle all sorts of situations without ducking out.

If you go to an agent expecting to be given an unending and uninterrupted flow of work, you may well be disappointed. Having delegated the search for work to someone else, you could end up sitting around, not working. If your contract doesn't allow you to seek your own clients, you might feel trapped. How you deal with this scenario depends on your personality type and the flexibility of the agency and its contract. (That said, most of the time there should be a practical way for both parties to work together to increase the flow of work, unless you are a particularly passive individual, in which case you probably shouldn't be operating as a freelancer anyway.)

Contracts   **>** Most artists seem to want an agent, but many then spend their time complaining about him or her. It's an interesting relationship. Very often the agent is seen as the boss, but it's the artist who pays the agent for his or her services. If the agent is in a superior role at all, it's one of management by consent. There are so many variables in this relationship, and much is dictated by the presence or lack of a contract that defines it.

There are agents who rely on contracts to tie the artists they represent to their agencies, rather than on the relationship that develops between them to create natural, mutually beneficial bonds. To look at the pros and cons of a contract, aside from any clauses that might tie one party to the other, we need to look at the kinds of relationship that develop between artists and their agents.

An agent taking on a new, recently graduated artist will need to spend a considerable amount of time, effort and money to promote this person. The result may be a huge runaway success or, more likely, a slow-burning interest that builds gradually and solidly. A substantial amount of investment goes into building the career of a budding illustrator in this way.

However, as in the showbiz cliché, the artist may up and leave once he or she becomes a glittering star, disregarding the work that was put into making them successful. An artist who assumes that his or her reputation has been built solely on the quality of their work is being naïve. I think it's natural and, from a business perspective, prudent for an agent to wish to protect themselves from this kind of caprice in some way.

The fearful or more cautious may opt for a signed contract that, in the event of a breakdown in the working relationship, will protect their business interests. Since an agency is the sum of its parts – i.e. its artists – if they leave there is no agency. If there is a contract that ties the artist to the agency, then the agency's existence can be protected. That's one way of looking at it.

An alternative way to approach this potential problem is to ensure that the agency runs well, provides good services, is fair and equable to its artists, and offers an environment that the artists would not wish to leave. Nevertheless, given that a very personal business relationship exists between an artist and his or her agent, even with the best will in the world things can go wrong. If the relationship with an artist deteriorates to such an extent that the differences cannot be resolved, I think it's probably healthier for both parties to part company, rather than be forcibly bound to each other by a contract. If an agency's survival is dependent on the retention of any one artist, then there is a flaw in the business model that is likely to prove fatal eventually anyway.

Contracts are the sum of what they say, so they will change from one to another. In the case of illustration agencies, they vary according to their clauses but roughly fall into two types. The first is the contract that you are expected to sign and so is clearly understood to be legally binding. It is usually exclusive, meaning that any work an artist does has to be conducted via the agency, and will cover a fixed-term period or last until termination by either party. The right to terminate a contract will vary from agency to agency, so check that part carefully.

If you have an agent in one country, the expectation is likely to be that all work for clients in that country will go through the agency. If a well-established artist signs up with an agent, there may be a proviso in the contract that allows the artist to maintain a specific list of clients as his or her own, but many agencies will have a strict policy that everything must go through them.

Signing up with an agent is usually territory-specific, so some artists have more than one agent. Before assuming you can sign up with several agencies – perhaps one in your own country, one in Japan and another in the US – it's always best to check how they feel about you being represented by another agent in a different territory. Conflicts can arise where there is any promotional crossover, and, with the web and the globalization of the industry, such crossovers can occur quite easily.

The second type of contract is more of an agreed outline of understanding between you and the agent. It will usually say what the commission rates are, what is expected of you and what you can expect from the agent. Signature on this type of 'contract' is unusual, but the basic premise is that these are the rules by which you both play, and if you break them, you may lose your representation. It does not necessarily tie you to the agent, but it should tell you clearly what you can and can't do with respect to working via the agency or not. It may have the same stipulations as an exclusive contract, but you aren't expected to sign up for, say, two years, with no option to end the agreement. We as an agency were once forced to buy someone out of an existing agent's contract. The artist was keen to leave the agency as she had not received much work in the preceding ten months, and it was felt unlikely that she would have done any more work in the remaining six months of the contract. Rather than accept a financial compromise dealing with any crossover because of existing promotion, which would have allowed the agency to earn some commission, the agency refused to let the artist in question leave. It struck me at the time as a rather self-defeating stance to take, and it unnecessarily soured all further relations that the agency was likely to have with the artist.

In today's information-rich environment, it isn't difficult to get an artist's direct contact details and bypass their agency. This forces many agents to rely on the type of signed contract discussed above that offers only 100 per cent

'Sometimes having an agent breaks the energizing link between me and the people who are asking me to create work ... I don't like to feel insulated from a client. The people who want my work are part of what drives me.'

Marc Boutavant, Illustrator

exclusive representation. Sometimes a client, having seen work that was done via the agency or having received promotional material sent by the agent, will make efforts to contact the artist directly. When the understanding established with the artist means that the job should be handled by the agency, the artist needs to honour that understanding. This is a matter of trust, whether a contract is in place or whether it's simply an agreed understanding with the agency. The artist who fails to honour the agreement is either in breach of contract or in breach of trust. If the relationship is defined at the outset, in writing, it can allow both parties to rely on mutual trust to abide by the terms of representation. Both artist and agent should respect each other, and I find this a healthier option than relying only on the constraints of a legally binding contract.

If you are the kind of artist who thinks an agent is there to take care of you out of the kindness of their heart, and who therefore resents any fees they charge for their services, you may not get the best from your agent. I knew an illustrator who bitterly resented hers because he bought his house in the country with 'her' money. Even at the time, as an illustrator represented by another agency, I felt this was a fairly skewed piece of thinking. On the flipside, some agents may take on any number of artists, each of whom they see as a 'cash cow', and will always find something the client wants at a price largely dictated by the client. The quality of the relationship is determined by the attitude and actions of both parties. It should be symbiotic, one of teamwork where both artist and agent work together towards mutually beneficial goals.

Agency promotional mailers

How to find the right agent for you

> Having looked at what agents do, and the pros and cons of having one, if you decide that you want agency representation you have to think about the kind of agent you need. The decision to be represented certainly isn't a unilateral one. Only when an agent has said he or she would be happy to represent you does the choice to go with them fall entirely to you. However, you can actively seek representation with the agency of your choice. I don't think looking for representation with 'any agent' is a good idea. It smacks of both a lack of judgement and also, possibly, a bit of desperation.

Finding out which agent might suit you and your work best is a matter of looking at who is available and assessing their suitability. Your local society of illustrators is likely to have a list of agents, and can sometimes supply further information on them. Asking your peers is often a good source of background information on agents, including their reputations and the esteem in which they are held by the illustration community. Word on how good, bad or inept an agent is usually travels far and fast on the grapevine. Searching on the web is an obvious way to look at agents, and perusing their websites will give you a good feel for the kind of work they represent and how they present themselves to the industry.

The first step is to look at the artists an agency already represents and the types of illustration they produce. Would you be happy to be presented alongside them or that kind of work? Do you think what you do would fit in well with that particular stable of artists?

How many artists does the agency represent? Do you feel you might get lost among them? Is the agency taking on new artists at the moment? If you get as far as speaking to them or being considered for representation, you could ask them about the maximum number of artists they will represent. It's useful to get an idea of how selective they are and whether they have an optimum number of artists they can realistically provide services to. As an extension of these questions, you could check on the number of people the agent employs to look after the needs of the represented artists. Do you feel confident or comfortable with this number?

Another clue to the culture of an agency can lie in the agent's professional background. What did they do before they were an agent? How did they become an agent and why? You may get a stock PR response, but you can usually get a measure of someone by how they answer these questions and justify what they are doing. In a similar way, ask about the background of the other staff. It's important, as it's likely that these people will be representing you and your work to potential clients.

When contacting an agent, whether enquiring about their submissions procedure or seeing if it's possible to get in to meet them face to face, approach them as you would a potential client. Like commissioning clients, agents are generally very busy so you will need to be clear and concise in your approach. If you send samples by post and you want them returned, be sure to make this clear and enclose a stamped addressed envelope for their return. As with clients, don't just e-mail a load of attachments because it's convenient for you to do so. Ask whether this is an acceptable form of submission and, if not, find out what they would prefer.

Meeting prospective agents

> After weighing up potential agents at arm's length, choosing the right one probably comes down to having a face-to-face meeting with them, and then to how you get on with him or her and any staff they may have. You need to feel that they understand your work, are interested in it and are sympathetic to what you want for it. You will be dealing with these people a lot if you end up being represented by them, so ideally you need to be confident that you can all get along. Yes, you could say it's primarily a business relationship, but by the nature of the work it usually ends up being more personal than that. I don't think I could represent someone I didn't like, regardless of how good their illustration was. I don't have to be best friends with them, but there does need to be a good flow of communication, respect, trust and goodwill for the relationship to work well – you will need to talk to each other about all sorts of things during the course of a working relationship, and so communication is an important consideration.

Of course, getting that face-to-face meeting isn't just down to whether or not you want to meet the agent. If they're busy, they need to be interested enough in you and your work to see you in the first place. What agents look for varies from agency to agency, but they have to believe they can sell your work, that there's a market for what you do.

Some agents will be looking for work that fits within tried and tested market parameters; others may be looking to put something new out there and to push the market to create a place for innovative work. How they find new artists will also vary. Some will proactively seek them at graduation shows and exhibitions of work, while others may be too busy and will simply weigh up the artists who come to them looking for representation. Each agency is different, so it's difficult to say what their individual criteria for representation actually are.

The questions you need to ask when you meet a potential agent should focus on how they do business. Who has the agency worked with? What kind of clients do they have? How do they go about getting commissions? Ask to see some of their promotional material. What do you think of it? Would you be pleased to appear in it? Is the work well presented and well printed, or does it look as though it's been done with little care – or with a lot of care but a 'bad eye' and a lack of flair? How do they present work to clients? Ask to see some portfolios. Are they well looked after, fresh, sharp and professional, or dog-eared, scuffed, untidy and generally not very well maintained? These are some very basic questions, and well-presented promotional material and portfolios are the minimum you should expect from a professional and well-established agent (even if their aesthetic isn't one you share).

Ask how the agency deals with client contracts. Do they take the fine print seriously? Do they sign on behalf of the artist, or do they expect artists to review and sign contracts themselves? Do they dispute certain clauses in these contracts? What is their general attitude, and how hard do they fight unfair clauses? Maybe ask how they deal with clients when things go wrong. Ask for some examples, perhaps including the best and worst possible resolutions.

What does the agency feel about such disputes, and what stance does it take when the problem stems from a client's unreasonable position? Unfortunately, occasions do arise where a client decides that they wish to kill a job and states (rather than agrees) a kill fee. My feeling is that one should judge the value of a client by how they deal with things when a job doesn't go according to plan. When everyone is satisfied, there is rarely a problem. On the rare occasions when you might need to agree a kill fee, whether the client plays fair is soon evident. If they agree one that leaves all parties happy, everyone can put it down to experience and move on. If a client, simply because they hold the purse strings, offers a derisory 'take it or leave it' kill fee, knowing that it isn't worth involving lawyers, you have a bullying client and have to question whether they are worth retaining.

Some agents may see the client as the most important person in the equation since, from a mercenary point of view, they represent potential work for many other artists. In this situation, the agent is likely to accept a resolution that favours the client at the artist's expense and you, in turn, should question where the agent's loyalties lie. Is their priority finding a fair and equable resolution to the dispute, or is it protecting their own income? For this reason, among others, you need to select your agent carefully.

The above questions are, to my mind, the primary considerations when deciding whether you would like a particular agent to represent you. The answers will give you a sense of the culture of the agency you are thinking of joining.

Costs and clauses > Next, you have the question of the fees and costs involved in being represented. What commission rates does the agency charge? Is it one flat rate or are there tiers of commission, rates for different kinds of work or for different fee levels?

What other costs are there? Does the agency charge for couriers, for the sending and returning of your portfolio to and from clients, for example? (Remarkable as it seems, some agents do charge for this, but I would say it's rare. The commission you pay should cover this kind of cost, so I would question any agent who tried to pass it on to you.) Are there charges for appearing on the agency website? Does it charge for updating images? Do you pay for portfolios or portfolio sleeves for the agency's copy of your portfolio? If there are promotional costs to which an agency expects all its artists to contribute, it should be able to tell you about them and give you some indication of what they will be. Do you have to pay for such costs upfront, or can they be set against income from work that you do via the agency?

Having been represented myself and now being in the business of offering representation, I would hazard a guess that most agents have upfront costs that they will expect artists to commit to. This isn't to say that these costs have to be paid immediately. I would say that most agents would want to assist a new illustrator they took on, and would most probably strike a deal to have the costs repaid over a given period from the income generated by the work they get him or her. In general, it's a flexible matter that an agent will try to work out with you, to help you get started. Thereafter, you may need to budget to meet any promotional costs that are likely to come up on a regular basis, be it for inclusion in annuals or in bespoke promotions created by the agency itself.

If an agency offers to represent you, it becomes a matter of your choice as well as theirs. If you are interested in representation by that agency, you need to look at how the relationship between you is defined. Do they have a contract that you have to sign to accept the terms of your representation? If they don't have such a contract, do they have something that at least sets out the terms of representation, so that you know how things work, what is expected of you and what you can expect of your agent? Everyone concerned should know the deal.

If there is a contract, ensure you read it carefully. Take it away with you so that you can study it and make pencil notes in the margins if there is anything you don't understand or are not happy about. If in doubt, get advice, even if this is an explanation of what a particular clause means, or whether the contract is reasonable as contracts go. Be wary of anyone who tries to get you to sign a contract in haste without giving you time to read it thoroughly.

Check what happens in the event of your wanting to leave the agency for any reason, or if the agency no longer wishes to represent you. If there's a contract, it's likely to be covered in there, but if not just ask. In the case of a contract, it's particularly important because if things don't work out, or you find you have misunderstood another point in the contract and no longer wish to stay with the agency, the clause that relates to terminating your representation may mean you are stuck for a given period of time, which could be two years or more. If you don't take the time to look at these things properly, what began as an exciting step in your career could end up feeling like a prison sentence.

Assuming there is a contract, after you've read it carefully, consider how your would-be agent deals with the questions that arise. He or she should be patient and explain any points you don't understand. If you have a reasonable concern about a particular clause, they should be willing to compromise (provided this doesn't undermine their position unreasonably) or at least explain why that point can't be changed. Once you have read, understood, discussed and considered the contract, you have to decide if you can work with it or would rather walk away. It's all you can do in any situation, and it is the same with client contracts. The worst thing you can do is just sign and live with the consequences. That really is a case of signing in haste and repenting (and moaning) at leisure. Whatever your decision, be sure that it is an informed one.

Conclusion > In spite of all the talk of draconian contracts and questionable practices, most artists' experience of working with agents is likely to be good. I've trawled through my memory banks of horror stories that people have told me about their agents, but I've had to dig very deep. I've been on both sides of the fence, first as an illustrator and now primarily as an agent, and my experiences have been predominantly positive. My own first agent approached me wearing a hideous suit and struck me as someone I couldn't imagine working with. In fact, he was — and still is — a decent and honest agent and one I'm very grateful to for all the help and support he gave me when I was starting out. The fact that I operate my own agency in a very different way doesn't diminish my respect for him.

In my role as an agent, along with my colleagues in both London and New York, I get a great deal of enjoyment, satisfaction and a sense of pride from helping new artists, and in many cases building up their confidence and belief in themselves. I've enjoyed fighting their corners when one or two clients have tried to behave unreasonably. Most of all, the relationship with the roster of artists we represent as an agency is one of respect, and, as with all agents, without this mutual respect the whole business wouldn't work, contract or no contract.

Bipolar by Aude Van Ryn, for *Therapy Today*

Brett Ryder

How well do you think your time at college prepared you for the realities of working as an illustrator?

> I studied graphic design and illustration at Camberwell College of Art – it was a secure bubble that protected me from the outside world. When it ended, the bubble burst and I came hurtling to the ground. I was saved by the net of the postgraduate course at St Martins, which was part-time and allowed me to dip my toes into the real world of illustration.

How did you begin to work as an illustrator?

> I seemed to spend a lot of time in newsagents looking for art directors' phone numbers, and thinking that working for newspapers would be the Holy Grail. When I started out, art directors were the masters of the universe, able to break you or create you.

How did you cope financially when you first left college?

> I went straight on the dole and stayed there for two to three years. I also had a part-time picture-framing job for four years.

Are you methodical in your working life, both in executing briefs and in dealing with day-to-day matters surrounding illustration?

> I'm comfortable with the creative side of my job and the overlapping of briefs, but the business side spins around me in a chaotic blur that I try not to get sucked into as I fear I won't be able to get out.

Do you work from home or a studio?

> I work at home, and always have done, originally to keep costs down and because I wasn't overly proud of my work and wanted to make my mistakes behind closed doors.

Do you have an agent?

> Yes. As I work from home, they are my main communication with the outside world. They listen to me and they get me work. Perfect!

What kind of promotional activity do you do?

> I usually send out a Christmas card to my clients, and every few years I produce a postcard for clients to remind them I'm still alive. I also have my own website, and the address is attached to my e-mails. My agency is always trying new ways of promoting me, rather than using the usual routes, and overall these have been very successful. With all new methods you will have successes and failures, but I'm happy to take those risks as it always makes things interesting.

What role do you think your website fulfils for you?

> It allows clients to see a wide spectrum of my work, and hopefully reassures them that I'm able to do their commission.

How would your working life change without an agent?

> I have had two continual strands running through my career: me and my agency. I wouldn't like it very much if either of them left.

Have you had any bad experiences with clients?

> A few. The worst was a job

I walked out of halfway through. The art director and I did not see eye to eye from the start. It was a painful experience.

Have you ever had disputes over getting paid by a client?

> Yes. I had been doing regular work for a weekly publication and was owed four months' worth of invoices, which the company said had been paid. In certain issues there had been two images but their computer system always only paid out for one. I had to show them all my invoices for three years, and my bank statements. It was very stressful, but they paid in the end – with no apology.

How do you feel about dealing with contracts?

> They're a pain for editorial jobs, but a necessity for bigger clients.

Have you ever turned work down for reasons other than not being available?

> Yes, if the client has an idea that I don't think my work is appropriate for.

What do you like most about being an illustrator? What do you like least?

> Making images. Doing accounts.

What is your prediction for the future of illustration?

> Computers inject a new lease of life into illustration. This opens up an infinite number of possibilities. It's a very exciting time.

What would be your advice to a new, would-be illustrator?

> Illustration is a precarious vocation, so you must always try to be honest with yourself and enjoy the work you're producing.

Above: *The Gene* for
The New Scientist
Right: *Fox and Hounds* for
The Times

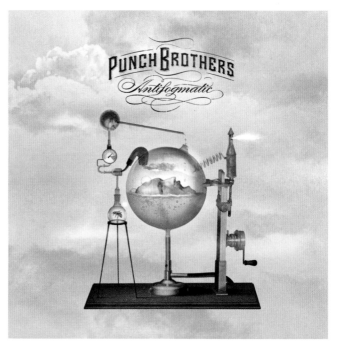

Above left: *The New Star* for
Brummell magazine
Above right: Punch Brothers
album cover
Left: *Cube Building*
Below: *She Talks to Animals* for
The Telegraph

Illustrators: Brett Ryder

The Good Boss for *Construction Manager* magazine

Appendix

Professional organizations

The Association of Illustrators
www.theaoi.com
info@theaoi.com
+44 (0)20 7759 1010
Information and support services
for new and established
illustrators in the UK – portfolio
tips, client directories, business
and legal advice, and more.

Dutch-illustration.com
www.dutch-illustration.com
info@dutch-illustration.com
Details on a selection of Dutch
illustrators, with images, links to
the illustrators' own websites and
e-mail addresses. Three or four
times a year an online exhibition
with a specific theme is organized.

Graphic Artists Guild
www.gag.org
membership@gag.org
communications@gag.org
32 Broadway, Suite 1114
New York, NY 10004
+1 (212) 791 3400
A national union of illustrators
and other graphic creatives in
the US, with classes and services
for members.

La Maison des Artistes
www.lamaisondesartistes.fr
For information on financial
assistance, legal advice etc.:
contacts@lamaisondesartistes.fr
Hotel Salomon de Rothschild
11 rue Berryer
75008 Paris
For information about
administration, social security,
subscriptions, billing etc.:
contact@mda-securitesociale.org
60 rue du Faubourg Poissoniére
75484 Paris cedex 10
La Maison des Artistes provides
advice on a wide range of issues
to artists of all disciplines, from
administration and legal advice
to promotion.

The Society of Artists
www.illustratorsagents.co.uk
21 Croftdown Road
London NW5 1EL
+44 (0)20 7424 0121
An affiliation of many of the
agents operating in the UK,
including some of the larger
agencies.

The Society of Illustrators
www.societyillustrators.org
info@societyillustrators.org
128 East 63rd Street
New York, NY 10065
+1 (212) 838 2560
Established society, with its own
gallery, promoting illustration in
America, organizing exhibitions
and lectures and providing advice.

The Society of Publication Designers

www.spd.org
mail@spd.org
27 Union Square West, Suite 207
New York, NY 10003
+1 (212) 223 3332
A professional body running annual competitions in publication design, including magazines, annual reports, brochures etc. Some, such as *The SPOTS Book*, promote illustration, while its main annual competition looks at image (both illustration and photo) and context design.

Tokyo Illustrators Society

www.tis-home.com
info@tis-home.com

Pages in the following books are available on payment of applicable fees. The page rates for each book vary and discounts are sometimes available for booking pages in advance or for the number of pages taken. Submission dates for the various annuals vary greatly, so it's wise to research the deadlines for bookings and submissions.

The Black Book

www.blackbook.com
eryder@blackbook.com
740 Broadway
New York, NY 10003
+1 (212) 979 6700 (x222)
An established and well-known American annual distributed to designers and art directors.

Contact

www.contact-creative.com
sales@contact-uk.com
+44 (0)1737 241 399
Promotional annuals for illustration and photography with wide distribution; inclusion by payment of fees. Includes online portfolios, repro services and printing and promotion.

Directory of Illustration

www.directoryofillustration.com
See also blog.directoryofillustration.com, with subcategories for different genres of work.

The I-Spot

www.theispot.com
support@theispot.com
+1 (800) 838 9199
Established US site with online portfolios for over 1000 illustrators from over 15 countries, along with stock illustration sales.

Le Book

www.lebook.com
info@lebook.com
4 rue d'Enghien
75010 Paris
+33 (0)1 47 70 03 30
French promotional annual for illustration, photography and fashion. US and UK editions of the book are also available via the local offices.

Le Book (UK)

info@lebook.com
43–44 Hoxton Square
London N1 6PB
+44 (0)20 7739 1155

Le Book (US)

info@lebook.com
552 Broadway, 6th Floor
New York, NY 10012
+1 (212) 334 5252

Medical Illustration Sourcebook

www.medillsb.com
Medical and natural sciences illustration, including animation and multimedia. Published in the US, with associated website.

Play!

www.playillustration.com
Illustration and design for toys and interactive games. See also blog.playillustration.com.

Annuals – Competitive

American Illustration

www.ai-ap.com
info@ai-ap.com
15 East 32nd Street,
7th Floor
New York, NY 10016
+1 (917) 408 9944
+1 (212) 408 9944
An established favourite.
Submission to the competition
for appearance in the book or on
their website (or both if you're
lucky) is limited to artists who are
working or are represented in the
US. Competition is fierce, but the
annual consistently showcases
the best of what is happening in
contemporary illustration.

Design & Art Direction (D&AD)

www.dandad.org
68–80 Hanbury Street
London E1 5JL
+44 (0)20 7840 1111
Worldwide design and art
direction competition, producing
an annual that features selected
examples of the best of the year's
design, advertising, illustration, TV
and environmental design.

Database suppliers

Agency Access

(formerly Adbase)
www.agencyaccess.com
sales@agencyaccess.com
275-S Marcus Boulevard
Hauppauge, NY 11788
+1 (800) 704 9817
+1 (631) 951 9500
Database of art directors and
art buyers, with custom-built
lists and mailing, marketing and
labelling services.

BikiniLists.com

www.bikinilists.com
+44 (0)141 636 9091
International (US, UK, Europe and
Australasia) database providing
mailing lists and marketing
services for the creative
industries.

File FX

www.filefx.co.uk
info@filefx.co.uk
7 Shepperton House
83–93 Shepperton Road
London N1 3DF
+44 (0)20 7226 6646
Marketing resource keeping
close tabs on who works where
in the UK creative industry.
Also provides lists for Europe,
North America, South Africa and
Australasia. Lists available as
online subscription, from which
you can create your own bespoke,
targeted lists.

Workbook

www.workbook.com
sales@workbook.com
940 N. Doheny Drive
Beverly Hills, CA 90211
+1 (323) 856 0008
Database and marketing services
for creatives, including a printed
book (with online version), online
portfolio service, mailing lists and
more, with offices across the
US – see the website for further
contact details.

Further reading

Business

These titles are business-oriented but full of tips that may come in handy. You don't need to take it all verbatim.

The Business of Illustration, Steven Heller and Teresa Fernandes. New York: Watson-Guptill, 1995

Graphic Artists Guild Handbook: Pricing and Ethical Guidelines, Graphic Artists Guild. New York: Graphic Artists Guild, 2010

Negotiating in a Week, Peter Fleming. London: Hodder & Stoughton, 2003

The One Minute Manager, Ken Blanchard and Spencer Johnson. London: HarperCollins, 2011

The Pursuit of Wow! Every Person's Guide to Topsy-Turvy Times, Tom Peters. London: Macmillan, 1995

Time Management in a Week, Polly Bird and Declan Treacy. London: Hodder & Stoughton, 2002

Creative

The Art of Looking Sideways, Alan Fletcher. London: Phaidon, 2001

It's Not How Good You Are, It's How Good You Want to Be, Paul Arden. London: Phaidon, 2003

The Medium is the Massage, Marshall McLuhan. Harmondsworth: Penguin, 1967 (and new editions)

Whatever You Think, Think The Opposite, Paul Arden. London: Penguin, 2006

Working: People Talk About What They Do All Day and How They Feel About What They Do, Studs Terkel. New York: The New Press, 1997 (new edition)

Inspiration

Artists and illustrators

Charles Addams
Karel Appel
Peter Arno
Charles Burns
A.M. Cassandre
Yves Chaland
Serge Clerc
Tony Cragg
Robert Crumb
Max Ernst
Fougasse (Cyril Kenneth Bird)
Francisco Goya
Ivon Hitchens
Hannah Höch
David Hockney
William Hogarth
Edward Hopper
David Jones
Anish Kapoor
King Terry (Teruhiko Yumura)
Len Lye
William Nicholson
Eduardo Paolozzi
Cornelia Parker
Robert Rauschenberg
Eric Ravilious
Dieter Roth
Miroslav Sasek
Jean-Jacques Sempé
Otto Soglow
Saul Steinberg
James Thurber
Edouard Vuillard
Tadanori Yokoo

Graphic design

Saul Bass
Seymour Chwast
Wim Crouwel
Alan Fletcher
Milton Glaser
Max Huber
Paul Rand
Paula Scher

Photography

Bill Brandt
Henri Cartier-Bresson
Gregory Crewdson
Walker Evans
Mario Giacomelli
Josef Koudelka
Dorothy Lange
Robert Mayne
Martin Parr

Films

A Couch in New York
  Chantal Akerman
The Last Detail Hal Ashby
The General Clyde Bruckman and
  Buster Keaton
Pickup on South Street
  Samuel Fuller
*Brazil / The Adventures of Baron
  Munchausen* Terry Gilliam
Animal Crackers Victor Heerman
  (Marx Brothers)
*North by Northwest / Rear
  Window / Vertigo*
  Alfred Hitchcock
Moby Dick John Huston
Ten / Close-Up Abbas Kiarostami
Hana-bi Takeshi Kitano
The Seven Samurai
  Akira Kurosawa
The Night of the Hunter
  Charles Laughton
Dog Day Afternoon
  Sidney Lumet
Duck Soup Leo McCarey
  (Marx Brothers)
*The Ladykillers / Sweet Smell
  of Success*
  Alexander Mackendrick
The Peddler / The Apple
  Mohsen Makhmalbaf
Badlands Terence Malick
*Dead Man's Shoes / This is
  England* Shane Meadows

The Battle of Algiers
  Gillo Pontecorvo
The Third Man Carol Reed
*Mean Streets / Goodfellas /
  Raging Bull* Martin Scorsese
*Mr Hulot's Holiday / Mon
  Oncle / Play Time* Jacques Tati
A Night at the Opera Sam Wood
  (Marx Brothers)

Books

L'Usage du Monde
  Nicolas Bouvier
The Master and Margarita
  Mikhail Bulgakov
*American Tabloid / The Cold Six
  Thousand* James Ellroy
Carter Beats the Devil
  Glen David Gold
The Tin Drum Günter Grass
Arguably Christopher Hitchens
Rogue Male Geoffrey Household
*The Lacuna / The Poisonwood
  Bible* Barbara Kingsolver
The Other Side Alfred Kubin
*The Honoured Society: The
  Sicilian Mafia Observed*
  Norman Lewis
Dreams of My Russian Summers
  Andrei Makine
The Giant, O'Brien Hilary Mantel
Moby Dick Herman Melville
Nonfiction Chuck Palahniuk
The Hawk Gil Scott-Heron
*Me Talk Pretty One Day / Barrel
  Fever and Other Stories /
  Naked* David Sedaris
*The Old Man who Read Love
  Stories* Luis Sepúlveda
*The Grapes of Wrath / Travels
  with Charley: In Search of
  America* John Steinbeck
Memoirs of Hadrian
  Marguerite Yourcenar

Websites

Mashable.com
News website and social media
blog. Covers the top social media
news from Facebook, YouTube,
Twitter, Pinterest etc.

TheOnion.com
Satirical news site covering US
and international news as well as
social and entertainment targets.

Acknowledgements

> I would like to thank Angus Hyland at Pentagram for suggesting me as a potential author for this book, and Jo Lightfoot at Laurence King for believing him and giving me this opportunity. When first approached, I felt that it was a subject that I could definitely write about, and I certainly felt the book was needed.

With no experience of writing books, I blithely assumed that it could be written fairly quickly over a few months. When it became evident it required an awful lot more work, my editor John Jervis was there to guide me through the lengthy process and ask the questions that I had omitted to ask myself. He was also the man to cajole and push me along the schedule. John also deserves a good deal of thanks for his patience in dealing with me.

I have to thank my colleagues at Heart, who took a greater burden of work on their shoulders in order to allow me to write. Helen Osborne took a firm hand in redirecting the workload, and Chloe Flynn and Amanda Mason both shouldered the extra demands without complaint. Without their support, this book would have been impossible.

Those who submitted to the interview process, the art directors and designers and the artists, are owed a debt of gratitude for their patience and generosity in sharing their thoughts on the industry, both for the purposes of this book and to help those who would be illustrators. I also want to thank Nicholas Blechman for agreeing to write the foreword to this book and for his belief in the project.

Finally, I'd like to extend a very belated thanks to two mentors who probably contributed to my ability to do what I do. A big shout and huge respect to John Furnival, who taught me at Bath Academy of Art and remains a good friend, and to Malcolm Winton, who was a breath of fresh air at the Royal College of Art. Malcolm, where are you now? Thanks to both of them for their nurturing, which was unquantifiable in many ways but gifted me the confidence to tackle almost anything.

Having taken time to address this second edition, I have once again to thank my colleagues at Heart – Helen Osborne, Chloe Flynn, Jenny Bull and Amanda Mason – whose support allowed me to work on the book.

I would like to thank the artists and clients who contributed their thoughts, time and work to the book. Thanks also go to Tom Gauld for his work on the new cover and chapter openers.

Thank you to Laurence King Publishing for the opportunity to update this book in full colour, and to my editors, Sophie Drysdale for getting me started and Clare Double for her patience and persistence in guiding me through the process.

Published in 2014 by
Laurence King Publishing Ltd
361–373 City Road
London EC1V 1LR
United Kingdom
Tel: +44 (0)20 7841 6900
Fax: +44 (0)20 7841 6910
E-mail: enquiries@laurenceking.com
www.laurenceking.com

Cover and chapter opener illustrations © 2014 Tom Gauld
Designed by Lizzie Ballantyne

A catalogue record for this book is available from the British Library.

ISBN: 978-1-78067-328-8

Printed in China.

Picture credits

Page 43 illustration © 2013 Bruce Ingman. From *Hooray for Bread*
written by Allan Ahlberg, illustrated by Bruce Ingman.

Page 44 above and centre illustrations © 2006 Bruce Ingman
Text © 2006 Allan Ahlberg
From *The Runaway Dinner* written by Allan Ahlberg, illustrated by
Bruce Ingman

Page 44 below copyright © 2010 Bruce Ingman
From *When Martha's Away* by Bruce Ingman

Page 45 illustrations © 2008 Bruce Ingman
From *The Pencil* written by Allan Ahlberg, illustrated by Bruce
Ingman

Pages 43–45 all images reproduced by permission of Walker Books
Ltd, London SE11 5HJ
www.walker.co.uk

Page 57 art direction by Leanne Addy, Marks & Spencer

Pages 61–62 © Marc Boutavant
Page 63 above © Editions Albin Michel/Marc Boutavant
Page 63 below © Millimages/Marc Boutavant

Pages 79–81 all © Michael Gillette
Page 79 above, *Thunderball* © Ian Fleming Publications Ltd 1961.
James Bond and *007* are registered trademarks of Danjaq LLC, used
under licence by Ian Fleming Publications Ltd

Page 97 art direction Ronn Campisi Design
Page 98 below art direction Nick Jehlen
Page 99 above right art direction Andree Kahlmorgan and
Emily Crawford
Page 99 below art direction Antje Klein

Page 116 art direction Jim Burke
Page 117 left art direction Jordan Awan and Chris Curry
Page 117 right art direction Chris Curry

Page 121 all and page 123 below, all images reproduced by
permission of Penguin Books Ltd

Page 132 illustration © 2012 David Lucas, from *The Skeleton Pirate*
by David Lucas. Reproduced by permission of Walker Books Ltd,
London SE11 5HJ
www.walker.co.uk